The Foundations of Paul Samuelson's Revealed Preference Theory

The Foundations of
Paul Samuelson's
Revealed Preference Theory

A Study by the Method of Rational Reconstruction

Stanley Wong

Routledge & Kegan Paul
London, Henley and Boston

First published in 1978
by Routledge & Kegan Paul Ltd
39 Store Street,
London WC1E 7DD,
Broadway House,
Newtown Road,
Henley-on-Thames,
Oxon RG9 1EN and
9 Park Street,
Boston, Mass. 02108, USA
Set in 10 on 12pt Times
and printed in Great Britain by
Western Printing Services Ltd, Bristol

British Library Cataloguing in Publication Data

Wong, Stanley

The foundations of Paul Samuelson's
revealed preference theory.
1. Consumption (Economics)   2. Samuelson,
Paul Anthony
I. Title
339.4'7   HB801   78–40600

ISBN 0 7100 8643 1

To my parents,
Elaine and Lang Wong

Contents

Contents

Preface and acknowledgments

It is my fondest hope that the present study will be seen as a contribution to a much-needed assessment of the significance of the revealed preference approach to the theory of consumer behaviour and of its heuristic value to economics in general.

This study is the product of a long period of unease and dissatisfaction with the theory of consumer behaviour which dates back to my undergraduate days at Simon Fraser University. Reflection on the conceptual foundations of the theory led me to Paul Samuelson's contributions to revealed preference theory (the so-called 'Samuelson Programme'). I soon became convinced that the Samuelson Programme is essentially methodological and that its success or failure depends on the validity of its underlying methodology. This line of enquiry, which generated as a by-product my 1973 article in the *American Economic Review* on the methodology of Paul Samuelson (see last paragraph in this Preface), has now resulted in the conclusion that the programme is a failure.

An earlier version of this study led to an award of a Ph.D. from the University of Cambridge. I wish to thank my supervisors for their advice and encouragement, especially for the freedom to pursue a line of enquiry which, in its earliest stages, appeared to be unmanageable and unrewarding: they are Professor Joan Robinson, Professor Luigi Pasinetti, Dr Lawrence Boland and Professor G. C. Harcourt.

I am greatly indebted to Joan Robinson, who by example and encouragement inspired this study. I am most grateful to Lawrence Boland for serving as the severest critic of my work; his incessant demand for clarity of thought has greatly improved this study.

I also wish to thank him for introducing me to the philosophy of Karl Popper and for suggesting that I use the method of 'rational reconstruction'. I owe special thanks to Geoff Harcourt for taking on the unenviable task of supervising a dissertation which was not initiated under him and for guiding it to completion. I also benefited greatly from the comments on various drafts of the entire manuscript from my colleague T. K. Rymes.

Since completing the original version I received much helpful advice and encouragement from Amartya Sen. My colleague D. G. McFetridge read the entire manuscript and offered useful suggestions for stylistic changes.

My excursions into the philosophical literature were aided by Alan Millar (University of Stirling) and Ian McFetridge (Birkbeck College, University of London). I thank them for helping me come to grips with difficult philosophical ideas.

I am indebted to the following individuals for their support, patience and tolerance during a difficult but exciting period of my academic career: Vicky (Becker) Wong, Fred Wong, Ed Wong, Mike Byram, Marie-Thérèse Byram and Mette Hoff.

The research embodied in this study was financed by a Woodrow Wilson Fellowship (1969–70), a MacKenzie King Travelling Scholarship (1969–70) and Canada Council Doctoral Fellowships (1970–1, 1971–2, 1972–3). I am grateful for the generosity of the sponsoring organizations. Also, I wish to thank the Institute of Economics, University of Copenhagen, for its hospitality during the academic year 1972–3. The preparation of earlier drafts was supported by grants from the Faculty of Social Science and the Department of Economics, Carleton University. I wish to thank Audrey Craig for her skilful typing and Jeremy Greenwood for proofreading help.

Parts of my article, 'The "F-Twist" and the Methodology of Paul Samuelson', *American Economic Review*, June 1973, vol. 62, pp. 312–25, are reprinted here with the kind permission of the publishers. An earlier version of this article received an Honourable Mention in the Stevenson Prize, 1971, University of Cambridge.

The book has been published with the help of a grant from the Social Science Research Council of Canada, using funds provided by the Canada Council.

Stanley Wong

Department of Economics
Carleton University, Ottawa

Chapter 1

Introduction

1. There is general agreement among economists that Paul Samuelson's research programme in the revealed preference approach to the theory of consumer behaviour was brought to a successful conclusion when Hendrik Houthakker (1950) proved the logical equivalence of revealed preference theory with ordinal utility theory.[1] This viewpoint, which was first expressed in Samuelson (1950b), owes its popularization to the influential survey on the theory of consumer behaviour by Houthakker (1961) (see also Arrow, 1967; Ekelund *et al.*, 1972; Katzner, 1970; Newman, 1965; Samuelson, 1963).

2. This research programme, which we shall call the 'Samuelson Programme', was launched by Paul Samuelson (1938a) in 'A Note on the Pure Theory of Consumer's Behaviour'. In an attempt to dispense with the concept of 'utility', as well as any other concept which does not correspond to observable phenomena, Samuelson proposed a new theory of consumer behaviour based on a postulate of consistency of behaviour. He believed that his theory, which is now known as revealed preference theory, succeeded in 'dropping off the last vestiges of utility analysis' (1938a, p. 62), because it consists only of observational terms, and therefore becomes amenable to empirical verification or refutation.

3. In Samuelson's opinion, the programme is further developed in 'Consumption Theory in Terms of Revealed Preference' (1948), in which the new theory becomes the basis for a method of constructing an individual's indifference map from observations of his market behaviour. This construction may be seen as an attempt to

1

make operational the concept of 'preference', i.e. to specify in terms of observable procedures the method by which an individual's preferences can be ascertained.

4. The appearance of the Houthakker proof provided Samuelson with the occasion to survey the achievements of his programme. In 'The Problem of Integrability in Utility Theory' (1950b), he proclaims that the goal of his programme is finally reached: revealed preference theory (as revised by Houthakker) is shown to be the observational equivalent of ordinal utility theory. The Houthakker proof, writes Samuelson, 'complete[s] the programme begun a dozen years ago [1938] of arriving at *the full empirical implications for demand behaviour of the most general ordinal utility analysis*' (1950b, p. 369).

5. This result, according to Samuelson (1953), implies that the choice between the two theories can be based only on the criterion of convenience:[2]

> The complete logical equivalence of this approach with the regular Pareto–Slutsky–Hicks–Arrow ordinal preference approach has essentially been established. So in *principle* there is nothing to choose between the formulations. There is, however, the question of convenience of different formulations (Samuelson, 1953, p. 1, emphasis added).

6. The proposition that the Samuelson Programme is completed has gone unchallenged in the literature. Moreover, there does not exist a substantive body of critical literature on the entire revealed preference approach. The criticism of non-specialists, such as Robertson (1951) and Robinson (1962), are largely ignored by specialists, while those by specialists themselves, such as Hicks (1974) and Georgescu-Roegen (1954a, 1973), are scattered in parenthetical remarks, footnotes, or book reviews. However, it must be pointed out that Sen (1973) devoted his inaugural lecture to an examination of the foundations of revealed preference theory.

7. Indeed the Houthakker result has become the point of departure for subsequent theoretical research (see, for example, Chipman *et al.*, 1971).[3] Moreover, it turned the (neo-classical) theory of consumer behaviour, by which is meant ordinal utility theory and its revealed preference equivalent, into a paradigm for economic theory in general. In the celebrated methodological dispute between Milton Friedman and Paul Samuelson, which was

settled in Samuelson's favour,[4] the theory of consumer behaviour was cited by Samuelson (1963) as the best example of an economic theory which has been developed to logical perfection. It is indeed surprising that in the time when fundamental issues are hotly debated,[5] the theory of consumer behaviour should stand out as one area in economics which is free from controversies and where the foundations are not subject to dispute.[6]

8. The current view is that the aim of the revealed preference approach is, and has been, 'to formulate equivalent systems of axioms on preferences and on demand functions' (Houthakker, 1961, p. 709). Notwithstanding Samuelson's position to the contrary, we can discern in Samuelson's writings at least three different and mutually inconsistent interpretations of the major problem to be solved by the new approach. This raises a problem of understanding the Samuelson Programme.

9. In Samuelson (1938a) the problem is to derive the main results of ordinal utility theory but without using any concept which does not correspond to observable phenomena. As a solution to this problem, Samuelson proposed a new theory of consumer behaviour. However, in Samuelson (1948) the theory becomes a solution to the problem of constructing an individual's indifference map. The first problem, it appears, is incompatible with the second. If Samuelson does solve positively the second problem, does this mean that he no longer finds objectionable ordinal utility theory? If so, does this not mean that the new approach was founded on an error, namely a misunderstanding of ordinal utility theory? Furthermore, since the second problem requires an antecedent acceptance of a preference-based theory of consumer behaviour, the alleged methodological advantage of the new theory is questionable. Is Samuelson's theory a new theory, i.e. does it represent a set of ideas which is different from those embodied in ordinal utility theory?

10. In Samuelson (1950b) we find a third interpretation of the central problem of the new approach. Here, it is to find the full empirical implications of ordinal utility theory, by which is meant the observational equivalent of ordinal utility theory. The third problem is incompatible with the first problem of developing a theory of consumer behaviour which does not rely on the concept of 'utility'. What is the point of seeking the observational analogue of ordinal utility theory if Samuelson intends to 'develop the theory of consumer's behaviour freed from any vestigial traces of the utility con-

cept' (1938a, p. 71)? If there is a positive solution to the third problem, the logical connection with ordinal utility theory is established rather than severed. Moreover, how can two theories be logically equivalent when one is considered observable while the other is not?

11. Samuelson has not addressed himself to these questions, nor has he realized that there are inconsistencies in his interpretations of his programme. Nevertheless, these inconsistencies are fundamental[7] and place in doubt the consistency of his research programme.

12. The aim of our study is twofold. First, we shall argue that Samuelson's contributions to the revealed preference approach do not constitute a consistent programme of research. Second, independently of the question of consistency, we shall argue that the Samuelson Programme is not completed because revealed preference theory does not solve any of Samuelson's three problems: the problem of deriving the main results of ordinal utility theory without the use of utility or any other non-observational concept; the problem of constructing an individual's indifference map from observations of market behaviour; or the problem of finding the observational equivalent of ordinal utility theory. This implies that the three major claims made by Samuelson for his new approach cannot be maintained:

(1) revealed preference theory is a new theory of consumer behaviour;
(2) revealed preference theory is an operational method for the construction of an individual's indifference map; and
(3) revealed preference theory is the observational equivalent of ordinal utility theory.

13. This study may be criticized for its narrow definition of the Samuelson Programme, namely the contributions of Samuelson to the revealed preference approach. Thus, even if the criticisms are correct, the study is of limited theoretical interest because more recent writers, for example Arrow (1959), Afriat (1967) and Richter (1966), have proposed satisfactory solutions to the three Samuelson problems. We strongly reject this assessment. As we shall argue in this study, the basic weakness of the programme is inherent to the revealed preference approach. It lies in the conception of the problems themselves. Therefore, the failure of the Samuelson Programme is of fundamental importance to the entire revealed preference approach and not merely of passing historical interest.

14. In comparison with most writings on the subject, Samuelson's contributions are the most illuminating, and are therefore worthy of careful study if we wish to come to a better appreciation of the entire revealed preference approach. Most writers ignore the interpretative aspects and focus almost exclusively on the mathematical structure of revealed preference theory. For example, the important paper by Uzawa (1960), which formalized the Houthakker result, is couched in formalism with a modicum of explanatory text. Samuelson, by contrast, not only created the theory and set out many of its theoretical propositions but also has given an interpretation of its significance and, moreover, has articulated the methodology which underpins the whole approach.

15. There is also a strategic reason why we focus on one writer. If we consider many different writers' contributions, there is the possibility that we may misconstrue those of any individual writer. It is therefore prudent to minimize this possibility by concentrating on the works of a single contributor. Therefore, except where stated otherwise, our criticisms of Samuelson do not necessarily apply to any other writer on the subject.

16. The Samuelson Programme has not been the subject of an interpretative study. Yet, its importance as a research programme cannot be denied. It lies not only in its continuing influence on research in the theory of consumer behaviour, but, more importantly, in its heuristic value for economics as a whole.

17. The birth of revealed preference theory is an event of great significance in the history of the theory of consumer behaviour. In the words of Arrow (1959, p. 121), it is 'the first distinctly novel approach' in the theory of consumer behaviour, long accustomed to the explanation of consumer choice in terms of preferences. With his new theory, Samuelson appears to attain the goal which eluded many economists in the past: namely, to sever the theory of consumer behaviour from the disciplines of philosophy and psychology, freeing the theory from the attendant controversies in which it has been enmeshed almost from its inception as a separate area of study.[8]

18. One of the first economists who expressed misgivings about the logical connection between economics and hedonistic psychology was Irving Fisher, who considered it an unnecessary source of controversy in economics.[9] To serve as the demarcation line between the two disciplines, Fisher (1892, p. 5) proposed the 'psycho-economic' postulate: 'Each individual acts as he desires.' This

strategy failed, because, as Sweezy (1934, p. 179) observed, it turns the interpretation of choice into a circular explanation, asserting that 'each individual acts as he acts'.

19. Another economist who tried to separate economics from psychology was Gustav Cassel (1918). Unlike Fisher he objected to the presence of psychological assumptions in economic theory, because, in his opinion, psychological phenomena do not fall under the purview of economics proper. While he considered the relation between psychology and economics to be worthy of further study, he did insist that in the explanation of prices only assumptions about demand functions are necessary as far as the demand side was concerned. This point of view never found a receptive audience,[10] despite Herman Wold's observation (1951; 1953, p. 63 and p. 329, n. 5) that the revealed preference approach is the modern legacy of Cassel's approach.[11] Samuelson, the originator of the revealed preference approach, certainly does not regard Cassel as his precursor. Instead, Cassel's approach earned the following comment from Samuelson: 'Cassel . . . rejected utility in favor of demand functions and nothing else, but was never fully aware of what he was thereby assuming or denying about empirical reality' (1950b, p. 366, n. 1) (see also Houthakker, 1961, p. 706).

20. Although the Samuelson Programme is considered completed with the Houthakker proof, it continues to exert considerable influence on the nature and direction of research in the theory of consumer behaviour. First, the revealed preference theory is now an established part of economic theory. Second, taking the Houthakker result as the point of departure, specialists have undertaken a systematic exploration of the logical relations between preference orderings and demand or choice functions under alternative formulations of ordinal utility theory and revealed preference theory. For example, Chipman *et al.* (1971) devoted an entire symposium to this line of enquiry, a line which was initiated by Uzawa (1960).

21. Outside the theory of consumer behaviour, the major impact of the Samuelson Programme is on methodology. Here, it enjoys a wider and, perhaps, more lasting influence in economics. The success of the Samuelson Programme has been attributed by Houthakker (1961) and by Samuelson (1963) himself to an underlying methodology which requires a scientific theory to be expressed solely in observational terms, devoid of philosophical elements. The importance of Samuelson's methodology is indisputable. A vast

majority of economists have adopted Samuelson's methodology to the point of regarding it as the scientific methodology appropriate to economics. This is borne out by the fact that in awarding Samuelson the Nobel Memorial Prize in Economics for 1970 the Swedish Royal Academy of Sciences cited him thus:[12] 'By his many contributions, Samuelson has done more than any other contemporary economist to raise the level of scientific analysis in economic theory.'

22. It is clear that our study depends fundamentally on the accuracy of our understanding of the Samuelson Programme and of its individual contributions. Accordingly, in chapter 2 we present and discuss in detail a method of understanding theoretical work. This method, which is known as 'situational analysis' or the method of 'rational reconstruction', regards a theory as a solution to a problem. To understand a theory is to conjecture the problem to which it is a tentative solution and to explain why the solution may be considered satisfactory, or otherwise significant, to the theorist. We propose to use this method throughout this study.

23. In chapter 3 we present an interpretation, along the lines of rational reconstruction, of John Hicks and R. G. D. Allen's formulation of ordinal utility theory. Its purpose is threefold. It sets up the background to which the Samuelson Programme must be compared, since Samuelson first proposed his theory as a replacement for ordinal utility theory. Second, it serves to illustrate our method of study. Third, it draws attention to a number of difficulties in the Hicks–Allen theory which warrant further investigation.

24. The core of our study is to be found in chapters 4, 5 and 6. Because we are evaluating the consistency of the various contributions to the Samuelson Programme, the problem of understanding the Samuelson Programme is partitioned into three problems. In chapter 4 we tackle the problem of understanding revealed preference theory as presented in Samuelson (1938a). In chapter 5 we examine the problem of understanding revealed preference theory as presented in Samuelson (1948). Finally, in chapter 6 we consider the problem of understanding revealed preference theory as presented in Samuelson (1950b). As a solution to each problem of understanding, we shall propose a rational reconstruction of the problem-situation of Samuelson. In addition, we shall criticize each (reconstructed) problem-situation from within and without.

25. Chapter 7 summarizes the results of our study. We conclude

with a rational reconstruction of our study, outlining a procedure by which our criticisms of the Samuelson Programme may be criticized in turn. This should be seen as a demonstration of the power and fruitfulness of the method of rational reconstruction in the study of theoretical work.

Chapter 2

Understanding and criticism

2.1 Introduction

1. Any criticism of a theory (or of a theoretical work, in general) is founded on an understanding of the theory. Because the validity of the criticism is to a large extent dependent on the correctness of that understanding, there is merit in making explicit the understanding upon which the criticism is to be constructed. This explicitness aids the task of criticism in two important ways. Where the criticism is valid, the critic can point out directly which parts of the theory are affected, which parts are left untouched, and, consequently, which parts should be replaced. Where the criticism is invalid, the critic or others can identify more easily the sources of the misunderstanding(s) that led to the invalidation of the criticism.

2. Our study of the Samuelson Programme is based upon solutions to two general problems: the problem of understanding any particular theory; and the problem of criticizing it. It is the purpose of this chapter to present our solutions to these problems. These solutions will then be applied to subsequent chapters concerning the investigation of the Samuelson Programme.

3. Our solution to the problem of understanding a theory emphasizes, above everything else, the objectives that the theorist, *qua* theorist, wishes to achieve. In other words a theory is interpreted as a solution to a problem, i.e. the creation of a theory is seen as being goal-directed or as a rational action.[1] We are therefore seeking to understand why the theorist regards his theory as an adequate response to the problem-situation as he sees it. The *problem-situation* or *logical problem-situation* comprises the objectives and their

9

logical interrelations. Thus, the problem of understanding a theory becomes a problem of understanding a problem-situation in the context of which the theory was proposed.[2]

4. The task of understanding a theory is to reconstruct the problem-situation of the theorist as he saw it and to show that, in his opinion, the theory is a satisfactory solution to the problem.

5. Our solution to the problem of understanding a theory is known as the *method of rational reconstruction* or the *method of situational analysis*.[3] It has been applied to the study of mathematical and physical theories, and to a lesser extent to sociological and anthropological theories. The application to economics is novel.

6. The striking feature of the method of rational reconstruction is the logical separation of the question of understanding a theory from the question of agreeing with it. As a consequence we can appreciate why the theorist considered his theory as an appropriate response to the logic of the problem-situation as he saw it, and, without any consistency on our part, we can also criticize the adequacy of the theory as a solution to the problem, or even the problem-situation itself. The importance of separating the two questions is derived from the fallibilist theory of knowledge due to Popper (1972, ch. 1). Its major tenets are that all knowledge is conjectural, that some or all of our knowledge may be false, and that even if it is true, it cannot be proven to be true. This position is not, as it may seem, one of despair or hopelessness. It countenances the possibility of improving our knowledge through criticism.

7. By contrast, there is a widely accepted, though mistaken, view that understanding entails agreement. It is said that if we can make sense of an action, we must agree with it; if we cannot, it must be irrational. Consequently, in the study of theories, the works of our predecessors are dismissed as irrational, or, at best, naïve.[4] Furthermore, this view denies the possibility of communication between those who disagree at the most fundamental levels. In short, to err is sin. The poverty of this stance stems from the failure to appreciate that all human knowledge, perhaps with the exception of mathematics and logic, is conjectural, and therefore fallible.

8. The method of rational reconstruction is not a psychological method.[5] It is not concerned with the psychological factors that may or may not have motivated the theorist. We admit that it is possible to give a psychological explanation, but we deny that a satisfactory explanation must be psychological. Psychological phenomena are

not the irreducible constituents of human actions because they may be further explained in non-psychological terms.[6] Although the processes of understanding may be psychological, the outcome is not; it is an interpretation, a theory. And theories and problem-situations are objects themselves; they are, in fact, the objects of our study.[7] Moreover, an interpretation (a theory) of a theory can itself be an object of investigation. For example, in chapter 7, we apply the method of rational reconstruction to our understanding of the Samuelson Programme. It will be an investigation into the history of historiography, the outcome of which will be a rational reconstruction of a rational reconstruction.

9. Our solution to the problem of criticizing a theory is to distinguish between internal and external criticism. This point of view is amenable to the method of rational reconstruction. Internal criticism is criticism within a (reconstructed) problem-situation. External criticism is criticism of the problem-situation itself.

2.2 The method of rational reconstruction

1. A rational reconstruction or situational analysis of a theory consists of two steps. First, we reconstruct hypothetically the problem-situation in the context of which the theory was proposed. In simple terms we are specifying the problem to which the theory is a proposed solution. Second, we explain why the theorist (or someone else) might think that the theory is a satisfactory solution to the problem.

2. The problem-situation comprises the theorist's objectives and their logical interrelations. The primary objectives upon which the theorist's attention is focused are called *theoretical aims*. They generate the main question(s) to which the new theory is directed. For example, in the Hicks–Allen theory of consumer behaviour, a theoretical aim is the explanation of consumer behaviour such that the corresponding question to be answered by the new theory is 'Why did the consumer buy a particular combination of goods?'

3. Apart from the theoretical aims, the theorist has objectives that form the background against which the main questions are raised. They are known as *situational constraints*. By placing restrictions or constraints on the choice of an answer (or answers) to the questions that express the theorist's aims, these objectives create the circumstance in which the theorist's problem arises, turning the questions

11

into a problem. Thus the *problem of the theorist* is to devise a theory that not only attains the aims but also satisfies the situational constraints.

4. It should be pointed out that there is no substantive difference between an aim and a constraint. This point of view is accepted implicitly by economists. For example, in the ordinal utility theory of consumer behaviour, it is said that the consumer's problem is to maximize utility (the aim) and to satisfy the budget constraint (the situational constraint). Alternatively, following the expenditure function approach of Roy (1942), we can say that the consumer's problem is to spend within his budget (the aim) and to maximize his utility (the situational constraint). Of course, the consumer's problem is conjectured by the theorist; it is different from the theorist's problem of explaining the consumer's behaviour, which, in turn, is different from our problem of understanding the creation of the theory.

5. For the purposes of our study, the situational constraints of a theorist's problem-situation are divided into the following categories:

(a)   an appraisal of theories relevant to the pursuit of the theoretical aims;
(b)   the general theory or theoretical framework of which the theory under study is an integral part;
(c)   the epistemological theory of the theorist;
(d)   the methodological theory of the theorist; and
(e)   the metaphysical doctrines of the theorist.

Because these objectives are background assumptions, and are therefore not always stated and/or apparent in the presentation of a theory, we shall explain why an appreciation of them may contribute significantly to the understanding of a theory.

6. Many theories are related to previous theoretical work. First, a theory may be addressed to questions to which there exist answers. In order to demonstrate the necessity for devising a new theory, the theorist usually assesses the existing answers by exposing their errors, omissions and other inadequacies. Second, a theory may be addressed to questions which are raised in the context of another problem-situation. It is an extension or further elaboration of some theoretical work. In other words the new theory is seen as a contribution to a programme of research. In this case the theorist

explains why the pursuit of his aims is compatible with the older problem-situation and how the attainment of these aims contribute to the research programme. Moreover, the older problem-situation and its solution will be a part of the situational constraints of the new problem-situation. For example, it is generally considered that the construction of an individual's indifference curves using revealed preference theory in Samuelson (1948) is a proper application of revealed preference theory as presented in Samuelson (1938a). Therefore, the problem-situation of Samuelson (1938a) and its solution form an important component of the problem-situation of Samuelson (1948) (see chapter 5).

7. Thus, from a theorist's appraisal of other theories, we gain important insights about the new logical problem-situation – the identification of certain constraints that are placed on the theoretical aims of the new problem-situation.

8. Often, a theory is an integral part of a general theory; it is contributing to a solution of a general problem. Therefore, the choice of a theory to attain the theoretical aims of the less general theory is constrained by the consideration that it must not conflict with the objectives of the general problem.

9. The theory of consumer behaviour is usually seen as a part of a more general theory, namely general equilibrium theory (GET) (see, for example, Pareto, 1909, p. 169, n. 1). In this context a satisfactory solution to the problem of explaining consumer behaviour must also contribute to the solution of the problem of explaining prices. Moreover, it must also be compatible with other solutions to sub-problems which contribute to the explanation of prices.

10. The importance of epistemology in understanding a theory seems questionable. Economists, with few exceptions, for example Georgescu-Roegen (1966, 1971) and Shackle (1972), do not acknowledge explicitly the relevance of the theory of knowledge to their endeavours. Notwithstanding this opinion, epistemology is important, if only because of its relationship with methodology which, as it will be apparent, has played a special role in the development of the economic theory of consumer behaviour.

11. The central question of epistemology, or the theory of knowledge, is 'What is knowledge?'[8] The traditional answer is that knowledge is whatever is provable or certain. We acquire (true) knowledge by proving our theories, statements, etc. Now, a statement is provable if it is deducible from some other statement or set of statements.

The demand for proof need not stop; the 'proving' statements themselves must also be provable. We reach an impasse. Unless we can stop this infinite regress of proof, we can never possess (true) knowledge since deduction only transfers truth, not generates it. From this a methodological question arises: 'What is the best source of knowledge?' The quest for knowledge becomes the quest for the source of knowledge. If a certain, secure foundation of knowledge is discovered, then all statements and theories which are anchored to this foundation will share that certainty, through the truth-preserving channels of deduction.[9]

12. Understanding a theorist's epistemological constraints helps us to appreciate the theory's differences from other theories. For example, we can contrast the two approaches to the theory of consumer behaviour by evaluating their epistemological assumptions. Utility theory, in some formulations at least, starts out from a set of fundamental axioms about preferences which are taken to be known from introspection or immediate personal experience. The self-evident truth of the axioms ensures the truth of the entire system (see Jevons, 1871, pp. 87–8; Robbins, 1935, p. 79). On the other hand, revealed preference theory is said to be based on a set of axioms of choice or observable behaviour (see Samuelson, 1938a; Little, 1949). Here, observation, being free from subjective elements, displaces introspection as the secure source. Although the two approaches differ on the choice of a starting-point, they both subscribe to the same epistemological doctrine, i.e. that making the correct choice is important.

13. An appreciation of a theorist's methodology, the theory of how to acquire (true) knowledge, contributes significantly to an understanding of a theory because methodological criticisms against an existing theory often provide a justification for the creation of a new theory. For example, two major developments in the theory of consumer behaviour grew out of methodological dissatisfaction with an existing theory. In accepting Pareto's proof of the immeasurability of utility, Hicks and Allen saw the need to replace Marshall's theory with their ordinalist revision. The impetus for the revealed preference approach, however, came from Samuelson's assessment that the ordinalist revision fell short of its goal of being an observational theory, though by replacing the concept of 'cardinal utility' with an ordinalist one, it moved in the right direction. Whatever the differences that divide the two theories, it is clear that

14

Hicks–Allen and Samuelson would agree on the answer to the methodological question 'How do we acquire knowledge?' For them, the answer is simply as follows: 'We acquire knowledge by making our theories observational because observation is the best source of knowledge.'

14. This answer to the methodological question blurs the distinction between epistemology, the theory of what is knowledge, and methodology, the theory of how to acquire knowledge. The link to which we drew attention is now forged. The epistemological quest for certainty merges with the methodological choice of a secure starting-point. An epistemological *cum* methodological doctrine emerges: knowledge is whatever is provable from observation.

15. Despite the fact that economists are generous in giving what is, in fact, methodological advice, they rarely recognize it as such. Consequently, explicit methodological discussions are dismissed on the grounds that they are not pertinent to the interests of economists. If a choice of a methodology must be made, and the practice is *de rigueur* in microeconomics textbooks, for example Ferguson (1972) and Green (1971), economists appropriate the methodology of some leading member of the economics profession. As Boland (1970a) has observed, economists, with few exceptions, can be divided into those who support the instrumentalist methodology of Milton Friedman (1953) and those who do not; this latter group, by implication, supports the descriptivist methodology of Paul Samuelson (1963, 1964, 1965a).[10]

16. Methodological debates are rare events, but a notable occurrence was the debate over Samuelson's methodology which took place in the 1964–5 issues of the *American Economic Review*. Unfortunately, the critics of Samuelson's methodology were reproached by Samuelson for attacking (Samuelson's account of) the methodology of the harder sciences.[11] A barrier to critical discussion was erected: any criticism of Samuelson's position is held to be a criticism of the methodology of the 'harder' sciences. It is not therefore surprising that there is little discussion on methodology, for economists, in general, are neither willing nor able to criticize the methodology of the physical sciences.[12]

17. The uncritical appropriation of a methodology is a commonplace.[13] In so doing, economists are unnecessarily restricting their freedom to choose a theory to attain their aims. But until they become aware that there are many more methodological options

than they suppose, methodological decisions in economics will continue to masquerade as applications of 'scientific methodology', of rules of formal logic, or of the theorems of mathematics, and so will be placed outside the scope of critical discussion.

18. Nevertheless, and notwithstanding the opinion of most economists, methodology does play a significant role in economics. It is a vehicle for the criticism of existing theory and for the creation of new theory. Accordingly, it must occupy a place in any attempt to understand a theory. In view of its part in the development of the theory of consumer behaviour, methodology forms, perhaps, the most important set of situational constraints in our study of Samuelson's problem-situations.

19. Metaphysics is that branch of philosophy which is concerned with the nature and existence of things. A metaphysical theory is a world-view; it concerns itself with the 'stuff' of which the world is made and the general relations that hold between the various phenomena, the existence of which it postulates.[14] This all-embracing character of metaphysics, not surprisingly, impinges on scientific endeavours. Metaphysics plays a regulative role in science, co-ordinating the choice of questions to ask and directing the search for answers to these questions. Generally, a metaphysical theory is not refutable, i.e. no possible event could conflict with it, or at least not allowed to refute it. The reason why a metaphysical theory is not allowed to be refuted is that it may serve as the scaffolding upon which empirical theories are constructed.[15]

20. Like methodology, then, metaphysics plays an important regulative role in the development and formation of scientific theories, placing requirements on what are considered satisfactory theories for the attainment of the theoretical aims. Unlike methodology, it makes factual assertions, assertions about what exists and about what the world is like. Methodology, by contrast, is about how to acquire knowledge about phenomena which metaphysics postulates to exist. Thus, in this sense, metaphysics is more fundamental than methodology.

21. Given its all-embracing, pervasive influence, metaphysics eludes any blanket definition. Instead of cataloguing the numerous definitions of metaphysics, our purpose is best served by considering a few examples of influential metaphysical doctrines.

22. The classical example of a metaphysical doctrine is the principle of causality or determinism: every event has a cause. It

asserts the irrefutable claim that the world is governed by strict natural laws with the consequence that an explanation of any event is unsatisfactory unless it includes strict natural laws.

23. Moving closer to economics, there is the metaphysical doctrine of the unity of mankind or humanism: all men are equal. The central problem that is generated in social science by this doctrine is how to reconcile the proposition that there are apparent differences among men with the idea of a common humanity.[16] As Joan Robinson (1962, p. 3) observed, its influence is felt in the moral and political spheres, setting out a moral standard for private life of treating others as we wish them to treat us and calling for a political programme of equal rights for all men and women. The unity of mankind theme and its associated political programme is clearly set out in the Universal Declaration of Human Rights, passed by the United Nations General Assembly some twenty-five years ago. Its first article reads as follows: 'All human beings are born free and equal in dignity and rights. They are endowed with reason and conscience and should act towards one another in the spirit of brotherhood.'

24. Psychologistic individualism, which became an influential doctrine in the social sciences through the works of John Stuart Mill and Vilfredo Pareto, asserts that all social laws can be ultimately reduced to psychological laws.[17] It is founded on the view that society and social institutions are merely manifestations of human minds, and therefore do not enjoy autonomous existence.[18] Pareto, who introduced the concept of 'indifference' to the theory of consumer behaviour,[19] subscribed to this doctrine of the primacy of psychology, but his metaphysics also included a mechanistic view of society. In advocating the reduction of all social sciences to psychology,[20] Pareto states unequivocally his acceptance of psychologistic individualism: 'La psychologie est évidemment à la base de l'économie politique et, en général, de toutes les sciences sociales' (1909, p. 40). Although his metaphysical doctrine is confirmed whenever some social phenomenon is explained in psychological terms, it is not refuted if any particular psychological explanation is refuted. The doctrine asserts only the existence of a psychological explanation for every social phenomenon. The search need never end.

25. General equilibrium theory, the currently accepted theory of price determination, may be seen to be regulated by the metaphysical doctrine of individualism that all social phenomena, for example prices, must be explained in terms of the behaviour of individual

agents.[21] This doctrine, like psychologistic individualism, is not refutable. If GET is refuted as a theory (explanation) of prices, there is no commitment to abandon the underlying metaphysical programme because only the existence of a particular type of explanation is asserted. Even though this research programme is not refutable, it may clash with certain empirical theories. For example, an explanation of prices in terms of group behaviour would be considered unsatisfactory.

26. The difference between the classical and neo-classical theories of distribution reflects some underlying differences in metaphysical outlooks (see Dobb, 1973, pp. 34–5). In classical economics income distribution is explained in terms of social institutions and social relations, while in neo-classical economics its explanation is a part of the theory of relative prices, since once the relative price of each 'factor' and the total quantity of that factor are determined, the relative share of that factor in total output is determined. For classical theory, in contrast to the neo-classical theory of prices, an explanation of income distribution is a precondition for an explanation of prices. This example highlights the sharp distinction between the metaphysics of the two schools of thought. Classical economics stress the fundamental importance of social institutions and social relations in the explanation of production and of prices. Neo-classical economics concentrate on natural factors – technical conditions, factor scarcities, and, in some formulations, preferences of individual economic agents – transcending social institutions and social relations.[22]

27. Our view of metaphysics as a regulative and co-ordinating agent is similar to what Schumpeter means by a vision, that 'pre-analytic cognitive act that supplies the raw material for the analytic effort' (1954, p. 41). A vision, for Schumpeter, is a precondition for theoretical development because it postulates what phenomena exist and the general relations that hold between them (1954, pp. 561–2):

> before embarking upon analytic work of any kind we must
> first single out the set of phenomena we wish to investigate, and
> acquire 'intuitively' a preliminary notion of how they hang
> together or, in other words, of what appear from our standpoint
> to be their fundamental properties.

28. In his study of value and distribution theories, Dobb (1973) draws attention to the important regulative role of a conceptual

framework, which, in his opinion, consists mainly of ideology, that historical-relative character of ideas. Although from our viewpoint, ideology is a part but not the whole of metaphysics, Dobb's description of the function of the conceptual framework aptly summarizes our views on metaphysics. The conceptual framework provides (1973, p. 19):

> the basis for suggesting and selecting questions for further enquiry, and hence for guiding future research and for bringing order into a mass of empirical observations that without more general concepts and hypotheses, depicting some pattern of interrelationships, would appear as uncoordinated and inexplicable.

29. Logic and mathematics are obviously part of a theorist's problem-situation. With one notable exception, Georgescu-Roegen (1966, ch. 2), economists accept without question the use of standard two-valued logic and mathematics. The problems intrinsic to these disciplines do not concern us here, though in principle they might. Our concern is with the applications of these disciplines to economics. Scrutiny and criticism of these applications will be undertaken, if necessary, in the discussion of the identified situational constraints of a problem-situation.

30. The above categories of the situational constraints of a problem-situation that is conjectured to be facing a theorist are by no means exhaustive. Keeping in mind that the purpose of a rational reconstruction is to solve the problem of understanding a theory, we identify and elaborate on those aspects of a problem-situation that we think is helpful to an understanding of a theory. This procedure is parallel to that in theoretical explanation. In ordinal utility theory, tastes and material circumstances (prices and income) are chosen as the explanatory factors. Implicitly, all other phenomena are regarded as peripheral to the understanding of consumer behaviour.

31. It is useful to distinguish between two types of solutions to a problem: positive and negative. A problem is solved *positively* if a solution is found that achieves simultaneously all the theorist's objectives. This is what is usually meant by a solution to a problem.

32. A problem is solved *negatively* if the solution states that it is impossible to achieve simultaneously all the objectives of the problem-situation. A negative solution is an admission of failure

19

but it can, nevertheless, be used as an instrument of learning. Arrow's 'general possibility theorem' (1951) is perhaps the best example in economics of a negative solution to a problem. In demonstrating the impossibility of having a social welfare function (SWF) that satisfies five seemingly reasonable conditions, he laid out the options that are open to those who are concerned with the construction of a criterion for social choice based on individual preferences. They have to give up the search for a SWF, devise an alternate choice criterion,[23] or change some or all the five conditions placed on the SWF.

2.3 Theory construction as problem-solving

1. Throughout the presentation of the method of rational re-construction, we characterized the activity of the theorist as one of problem-solving, which comprises aims, situational constraints and tentative solutions. Moreover, our activity of understanding the activity of the theorist, *qua* theorist, can also be brought under this general scheme. Our aim is to understand the creation of the theory; our constraint set includes in part the epistemological doctrine that knowledge is conjectural, the metaphysical doctrine that we should pursue true knowledge, and the view that we should be faithful to the documentary evidence.

2. Although structurally similar, the two activities are logically distinct. The objects of the two studies differ. The theorist is studying the behaviour of the consumer, while we are studying the behaviour of the theorist. Our study is a meta-theoretical study; our problem-situation is a meta-problem-situation. Thus, in principle, there are no problems common to both levels, as is also the case between a study of consumer behaviour and the behaviour of the consumer.

3. Nevertheless, a rational reconstruction (our meta-theoretical study) can contribute to the solution of the theorist's problem. It may show that the theorist's problem is unsolvable or that the solution is unsatisfactory because the theorist had misrepresented the actual situation facing him (Popper, 1968b, p. 179, emphasis added):

> It would be a task for situational analysis to distinguish between the situation as the agent saw it, and the situation as it was (both, of course, conjectured). *Thus the historian of science not*

only tries to explain by situational analysis the theory proposed by a scientist as adequate, but he may even try to explain the scientist's failure.

4. The characterization of theory construction and meta-theory construction as problem-solving should come as no surprise to an economist. The theory of problem-solving is similar to the theory of 'linear' programming – a theory that has found wide application in economics. On this analogy, a theorist (or a meta-theorist) is trying to 'maximize' his objective function (his aims), subject to the set of situational constraints. The theorist's solution is an optimizing solution, provided that the programme has a solution.

2.4 Criticism of the method of rational reconstruction

1. Our method of understanding a theory, as with all aspects of the study, is open to critical discussion. Probably, the major objections to this method are that a rational reconstruction is conjectural, and therefore it may be a distortion of real history and, further, that conjectures do not follow from the evidence that is available in the writings of the theorist under study.

2. The first objection is not specific to our method, or to the study of theories. All attempts at historical understanding have the character of being conjectural, as are all attempts at theoretical understanding in general. For example, in the ordinal utility theory it is conjectured that the problem of a consumer is to maximize his utility subject to his budget constraint.

3. The second objection follows from the first: that history should always follow from the available evidence. Our task is to understand the activity of the theorist, *qua* theorist. If we do no more than report the facts, we shall contribute very little. Explanation, by its very nature, goes beyond a redescription of the facts; explanation is always under-determined by the behavioural evidence.

4. In section 2.1 above, we explained that the method of rational reconstruction permits the historian of ideas to separate logically the question of understanding a theory from the question of agreeing with it. This consideration was the decisive factor in choosing a method for the study of the Samuelson Programme. There is also a contributing factor. The alternatives to this method are unsatisfactory. In the study of the theory of consumer behaviour, three types of studies figured most prominently: accounts that concentrate

on biographical or priority information; those that are written from the standpoint of particular technical interest; and those that are written from the standpoint of currently accepted theory.

5. In the main, biographical and priority information are recounted in textbooks on economic theory. Unfortunately, this emphasis does not allow the historian of ideas to account for the development of new theoretical constructs – a central interest in the study of theories. For example, the fact that Edgeworth (1881) introduced the indifference map into economics does not help to explain why that construct became widely used with Hicks and Allen (1934) some fifty years after its introduction: 'Why . . . did it take more than fifty years for the means of a notable advance to be fully exploited?' (Shackle, 1967, p. 10).

6. On the other hand, surveys written from a particular technical interest are too restrictive. By focusing only on those aspects that pertain to this interest, they present an abbreviated history of a theorist's contributions (see, for example, Brown and Deaton, 1972).

7. What is especially pernicious is 'revisionist history'. For revisionist historians, currently received theory is taken to be superior to earlier theories. Consequently, these earlier theories are studied and evaluated in the light of contemporary theory. Distortions inevitably result because, for these historians, the value of earlier theories lies solely in their contributions to contemporary theoretical questions and problems. For example, consider Samuelson's brief but influential account of the history of consumer theory (1938c, 1947). In his opinion all major contributions in the theory have been part of a movement away from psychological and philosophical connotations. This interpretation overlooks the specific philosophical import of individual theories. For example, Jevons (1871) considered his economic theory to be an application of utilitarian calculus, while Pareto (1909) was concerned with the development of economic theory as a part of a wider programme in the social sciences, that of reducing all social theories to psychology.

2.5 A solution to the problem of criticism

1. Having set out our solution to the problem of understanding a theory, we shall now propose a solution to the problem of criticizing a theory, that is, more precisely, a rational reconstruction of it.

2. Criticism, in our opinion, is an integral part of the activity of

problem-solving. From the standpoint that all knowledge is conjectural, criticism is an instrument for improving our knowledge through the elimination of error.[24] By bringing severe criticisms to bear on our conjectures, we can alleviate, though not overcome, the limitations of our knowledge.

3. Our solution to the problem of how to criticize is to divide criticism of a theory (our rational reconstruction of it) into two categories: internal and external.[25] Internal criticism is criticism within the context of the (reconstructed) problem-situation, i.e. we are accepting the theorist's aims and constraints without dispute. It consists by and large of criticisms of the validity of logical and mathematical arguments. Since logical and mathematical theories are usually accepted in economics without question, internal criticism of this type is easily accepted by protagonists in a debate.

4. In addition, internal criticism includes evaluation of the consistency of the various objectives of the theorist and of the consistency of the (tentative) solution with the theoretical aims and constraints. Criticism of this type is the most devastating. The inconsistency of the objectives implies that the problem is unsolvable. The violation of a situational constraint by a proposed solution gives sufficient grounds for rejecting the solution.

5. External criticism, on the other hand, is criticism from outside the (reconstructed) problem-situation. In this category fall criticisms of the importance of the problem, of the accuracy of the theorist's representation of the situational constraints facing him and of the objectives themselves.

6. The importance of a problem may be assessed from various standpoints. For example, a problem may be dismissed on moral grounds if its consideration would be incompatible with certain moral beliefs of the critic; or a charge of irrelevance may be levelled against a problem if it lies outside the critic's general field of interest.[26]

7. Heated debates are generated over a theorist's account of the situational constraints facing him. In particular, interpretations of theories and reports of economic events are often the subject of countless exchanges of criticism and counter-criticism. In these debates a conclusion acceptable to all sides is rarely found or expected.

8. More generally, individual objectives may be criticized. For example, if a theory is part of a more general theory, external

criticism would be criticism of the general theory. A theorist's methodology may be examined on its internal consistency; it may be the object of a sub-problem of understanding.

9. The point of distinguishing between internal and external criticism is that all criticisms are not interdependent. Some critical remarks can be accepted without a concomitant obligation to accept others. Successful counter-criticism does not therefore entail the refutation of all critical remarks. Furthermore, the difficulty in resolving disputes which are generated by external criticism on values, ideology, metaphysics and methodology will not be allowed to spill over into the arena of logical and mathematical arguments of internal criticism – where conflict-resolution is relatively easier.

Chapter 3

The Hicks and Allen Programme

3.1 Introduction

1. In 'A Reconsideration of the Theory of Value' (1934) John Hicks and R. G. D. Allen revise Alfred Marshall's theory of consumer behaviour on ordinalist lines. In each place where a measurable concept of utility is used in Marshall's theory, they substitute in its place an ordinal concept of utility; for the cardinally measurable utility function, they substitute an ordinal utility function or a scale of preferences (which is represented by an indifference map), and for the 'law of diminishing marginal utility', they substitute the 'law of increasing (which later became known as "diminishing") marginal rate of substitution'. In the opinion of Hicks and Allen, the revision is necessitated by Pareto's proof of the immeasurability of utility. They observe that although Pareto (1909, p. 168 and *passim*) introduced indifference curves into consumer theory, he failed to reformulate his consumer theory solely in ordinalist terms (see Hicks and Allen, 1934, pp. 196–7).

2. The importance of understanding the Hicks–Allen theory in a study of the Samuelson Programme is that Samuelson's decision to create a new theory can be attributed to a dissatisfaction with ordinal utility theory. In Samuelson's opinion, ordinal utility theory fails to become an observational theory, one which is to be free from the philosophical and psychological controversies in which utility theory had been enmeshed throughout its history (1938a, pp. 61–2):

> Hence, despite the fact that the notion of utility has been repudiated or ignored by modern theory, it is clear that much of even the most modern analysis shows vestigial traces of the

25

utility concept. Thus, to any person not acquainted with the history of the subject, the exposition of the theory of consumer's behaviour in the formulation of Hicks and Allen would seem indirect. The introduction and meaning of the marginal rate of substitution as an entity independent of any psychological, introspective implications would be, to say the least, ambiguous, and would seem an artificial convention in the explanation of price behaviour.

It is thus fitting to begin a study of the Samuelson Programme with an interpretation of ordinal utility theory, for, if we are to evaluate whether or not revealed preference theory succeeds in avoiding the pitfalls of ordinal utility theory, we must have an understanding of ordinal utility theory which is developed independently of Samuelson's interpretation of that theory. And a study of the Hicks–Allen theory would be sufficient for our purposes since some of Samuelson's objections against ordinal utility theory are directed at the Hicks–Allen theory.[1]

3. Thus we present a rational reconstruction of the Hicks–Allen Programme. Its purpose is threefold. First, it sets up the background to the Samuelson Programme. Second, it illustrates our method of understanding a theory through an application to a well-known theory. Third, it draws attention to a number of theoretical difficulties in the Hicks–Allen Programme that warrant further investigation.

3.2 The problem-situation of the Hicks–Allen theory

1. An understanding of the Hicks–Allen theory of consumer behaviour requires an appreciation of the problem to which it is a proposed solution. The problem for Hicks and Allen is to revise Marshall's theory of consumer behaviour without the use of an immeasurable concept of utility.

2. In Marshall's theory a consumer is motivated by the pursuit of utility which can be acquired through the consumption of goods. The amount of utility that can be derived from the consumption of any single good is subject to the law of satiable wants, i.e. the law of diminishing marginal utility (1920, III, III, 1):

> the additional benefit which a person derives from a given
> increase of his stock of a thing diminishes with every increase
> in the stock that he already has.

In addition, in a given time with given material resources, the marginal utility of money to a consumer is constant.

3. According to Marshall a consumer chooses a particular combination of goods with his income and at a set of prices that he cannot affect such that the marginal utility of each good divided by its price is the same for all goods. Contrariwise, if the ratio of marginal utility to price is not the same for all goods bought, total utility can be increased by purchasing more of those goods which have a higher ratio of marginal utility to their price. Since the law of diminishing marginal utility applies to all goods, the marginal utility of those goods, the purchase of which has increased, will decrease. The adjustment of expenditure will cease when the ratio of marginal utility to price is the same for all goods (1920, III, V, 2):

> And in a money-economy, good management is shown by so adjusting the margins of suspense on each line of expenditure that the marginal utility of a shilling's worth of goods on each line shall be the same.

4. From Marshall's theory the 'law of demand' can be derived, i.e. the proposition that the quantity demanded of a good is inversely related to its price, *ceteris paribus*. Assume that a consumer is maximizing utility. Then the price of each good bought is equal to the ratio of its marginal utility to the marginal utility of money – a constant. If the price of one good increases while all other prices do not change, then the marginal utility of that good must increase if utility is to be at its maximum. Given the law of diminishing marginal utility, marginal utility will increase if less of that good is purchased. Thus, if the price of a good increases (decreases), less (more) of that good will be demanded.

5. In Marshall's theory of consumer behaviour, utility is conceived as a quantitatively measurable concept. The use of this concept is declared illegitimate by Hicks and Allen because Pareto proved that utility is immeasurable from observations of behaviour: '[Pareto proved] that the facts of observable conduct make a scale of preferences capable of theoretical construction ... but they do not enable us to proceed from the scale of preference to a particular utility function' (Hicks and Allen, 1934, p. 52). The acceptance of this proof compels them to revise Marshall's theory because, in their opinion, concepts must be observational, i.e. correspond to observable phenomena. The task of revising subjective value theory, of

27

which Marshall's theory is one version, is left undone by Pareto, who failed to reformulate his theory of consumer behaviour in light of his proof: '[The task of the present paper] is the more pedestrian one of examining what adjustments in the statement of the marginal theory of value are made necessary by Pareto's discovery' (Hicks and Allen, 1934, p. 54).

6. Apart from the assumption that utility is measurable, Hicks and Allen do not voice any other objections against Marshall's theory.[2] It seems that they find the rest of Marshall's problem-situation unobjectionable.

7. The theoretical aims of Hicks and Allen are those of Marshall: the explanation of consumer behaviour and of the law of demand. Marshall's general analytical framework is individualistic. His explanation of consumer behaviour forms the basis of an explanation of market demand and market price. Hicks and Allen retain this individualism, which requires that all social phenomena must be explained in terms of individual behaviour. This is evident in Hicks (1939), in which the explanation of individual behaviour is a necessary step in the explanation of market demand (p. 34, emphasis added):

we have been concerned with the behaviour of a single individual. But economics is not, in the end, much interested in the behaviour of single individuals. Its concern is with the behaviour of groups. *A study of individual demand is only a means to the study of market demand.*

Furthermore, the explanation of market demand is integrated into a general theory of price which, it should be pointed out, follows in the tradition of Walras and Pareto rather than of Marshall. The importance of the constraint of individualism to the Hicks–Allen problem-situation is that any proposal to alter the theory will have to be examined on its implications for the general theory of price.

8. Marshall's individualism is psychologistic.[3] Individual behaviour is explained in terms of the individual's psychology; social phenomena are therefore explained in terms of individuals' psychology. The preponderance of such terms as 'desires', 'motives', 'aspirations', 'human nature' and 'utility' in Marshall's explanations of human actions attests to this (1920, I, II, 1):

[Economics] concerns itself chiefly with those desires, aspirations and other affections of human nature, the outward

manifestations of which appear as incentives to action in such
a form that the force or quantity of the incentives can be
estimated and measured with some approach to accuracy . . .

However, Marshall's adherence to psychologism is qualified; he
countenanced that an individual's tastes may be influenced by his
behaviour (1920, III, III, 2).

9. Likewise, the Hicks–Allen theory is psychological.[4] The
behaviour of a consumer is explained in terms of his preferences,
tastes, desires, wants, etc., which all refer to the individual's state of
mind. Hicks's and Allen's objection to cardinal utility is not that it is
a psychological concept but that it does not correlate with observable
phenomena (Hicks, 1939, p. 18):

'Given wants' can be quite adequately defined as a given *scale
of preferences*; we need only suppose that the consumer has
a preference for one collection of goods rather than another, not
that there is ever any sense in saying that he desires the one
collection 5 per cent more than the other, or anything like that.

10. The fundamental importance of psychological concepts to
the Hicks–Allen analysis is apparent. Changes in consumer behaviour
are attributed to changes in the conditions external to the consumer
under study. Thus (Hicks, 1956, p. 5):

The human individual only comes into plain economics as an
entity which reacts in certain ways to certain stimuli; all that
the Plain Economist needs to be interested in are the laws of
his reactions.

The link between external changes and changes in the consumer's
behaviour is preferences (tastes), which, for Hicks and Allen, are
assumed to be given and unchanging.[5] The strict independence of
preferences from conditions external to the consumer is emphasized
in part II of *Value and Capital*, in which Hicks comments on the
applicability of indifference analysis, the formal structure of his
theory of consumer behaviour, to other areas (Hicks, 1939, p. 55):

The objects bought and sold need not be consumers' goods, or
they need not all be consumers' goods; the necessary condition
is only that they should be objects of desire, which can be
bought and sold, and which can be arranged in an order of
preference (an indifference system) *which is itself independent of
prices*.

29

11. In summary, the problem-situation of Hicks and Allen is to revise Marshall's theory of consumer behaviour. The explanation of consumer behaviour and the law of demand are to be given within the framework of psychologistic individualism but without the use of an immeasurable concept of utility.

3.3 The Hicks–Allen solution

1. The Pareto proof of the immeasurability of utility is important in two ways for the Hicks–Allen Programme. First, it provided a sufficient reason for rejecting Marshall's theory, and thereby delimited the class of possible replacements. Second, it suggested the solution to the problem of revising Marshall's theory. In the course of setting out his proof, Pareto showed that a scale of preferences can be constructed from the facts of observable conduct. However, he never exploited this idea to its fullest. In the hands of Hicks and Allen, the concept of a scale of preferences becomes the basis for a new theory of consumer behaviour, the solution to the problem of revising Marshall's theory.

2. In the Hicks–Allen theory, a scale of preferences (an ordinal utility function) depicts the individual's tastes. First, it is assumed that a consumer's preferences are defined over all possible bundles of goods. Given any two bundles, he prefers one to the other or else he is indifferent. The locus of those bundles which have the same rank define an indifference surface; the indifference surfaces together make up an indifference map. Second, he prefers more goods to less goods. Given any two bundles, he prefers one to the other if it contains more of at least one good and no less of all other goods. Third, his preferences are consistent in the sense that if he prefers one bundle to a second he does not prefer the second to the first, and that if he prefers one bundle to a second, the second to a third bundle, he prefers the first bundle to the third. Fourth, his preferences exhibit a diminishing marginal rate of substitution throughout. This property is known as the 'law of diminishing marginal rate of substitution': the more good x_1 that is substituted for good x_2, such that the consumer maintains the same level of satisfaction, the less will be the amount of x_2 which will be given up for successive amounts of x_1.

3. In the Hicks–Allen theory, the actions that a consumer may take to fulfil his desires are limited by certain material conditions

external to him. These conditions are represented by the budget constraint, which determines the bundles that he may purchase with his money income at a set of prices which he cannot influence. In Shackle's words (1967, p. 80):

> Price generalizes the obstacles, giving to each participant of the market, in effect, a knowledge of the whole field of possibilities and enabling him to profit by the desires and consequent potential conduct of every one else.

4. In the Hicks–Allen theory, the explanation of consumer behaviour is effected by bringing together the description of the individual's tastes, the indifference map, with the description of the material circumstances confronting the individual, the budget constraint. The link between the two parts is established by the assumption that the individual seeks to maximize his satisfaction or utility, which is now conceived as an ordinal concept. Thus the action of the consumer, *qua* consumer, is seen as the outcome of the confrontation of tastes and the obstacles to their fulfilment. The explanation of consumer behaviour, of why a consumer bought what he did, is that, given his income and market prices, he bought the bundle which was the highest on his scale of preferences; all other bundles were not bought because they were either too expensive or were lower on the scale of preferences.

5. The explanation of the law of demand is more complicated. Since changes in the actions of a consumer, *qua* consumer, are attributed to changes in the material circumstances, a change in the price of a good will result in a change in the quantity of that good demanded. Consider, for example, the effect on the quantity demanded of good x_1 of a decrease in the price of that good, p_1. The quantity demanded of good x_1 will change for two reasons. First, as a consequence of the law of diminishing marginal rate of substitution, more of good x_1 will be bought because it is now relatively cheaper. This is known as the 'substitution effect'. Second, the quantity demanded of good x_1 will change because the real income of the consumer has increased. This is known as the 'income effect'. Whether there will be an increase or a decrease in the quantity of that good demanded is unknown in the Hicks–Allen theory. Thus the net result of the two effects together is not discernible in the Hicks–Allen theory; but, because the cases in which the income effect is negative and outweighs the substitution effect are examples

of Giffen goods, which are empirically rare occurrences, the quantity demanded of good x_1 will increase (decrease) when the price of x_1 decreases (increases) (Hicks, 1939, p. 35):

> Thus, as we might expect, the simple law of demand – the downward slope of the demand curve – turns out to be almost infallible in its working. Exceptions to it are rare and unimportant.

6. The Hicks–Allen theory can be expressed in a mathematical form in which the behaviour of the consumer is described as the outcome of a constrained maximization problem:

$$\max U = f(x_1, \ldots, x_n) + \lambda(I - \Sigma p_i x_i). \tag{3.1}$$

The first-order conditions are:

$$U_i = f_i - \lambda p_i = 0, \qquad i = 1, \ldots, n \tag{3.2}$$
$$U_\lambda = I - \Sigma p_i x_i = 0$$

and the second-order conditions are such that the bordered Hessian determinants alternate in sign, beginning with positive:

$$\mid \bar{H}_2 \mid > 0; \mid \bar{H}_3 \mid < 0; \mid \bar{H}_4 \mid > 0; \ldots \tag{3.3}$$

where

$$\mid \bar{H} \mid = \begin{vmatrix} 0 & -p_1 & -p_2 & \ldots & -p_n \\ -p_1 & U_{11} & U_{12} & \ldots & U_{1n} \\ -p_2 & U_{21} & & & \\ & \cdot & \cdot & & \\ & \cdot & \cdot & & \\ & \cdot & \cdot & & \\ -p_n & U_{n1} & & & U_{nn} \end{vmatrix} \tag{3.4}$$

From (3.2) we can, by solving for $x_i, \ldots, x_n$, derive the demand functions:

$$x_i = h^i(p_1, \ldots p_n, I), \qquad i = 1, \ldots, n. \tag{3.5}$$

7. By total differentiation of (3.2) and solving for $dx_1, \ldots, dx_n$, $d\lambda$, we can express the effect on quantity demanded of x_i due to a change in p_i as

$$(\delta x_i / \delta p_i) = (\delta x_i / \delta p_i)_{U=U_0} - x_i(\delta x_i / \delta I). \tag{3.6}$$

(3.6) will have a positive value if and only if

$$(\delta x_i / \delta I) < 0 \tag{3.7}$$

and

$$\mid x_i(\delta x_i / \delta I) \mid > \mid (\delta x_i / \delta p_i)_{U=U_0} \mid. \tag{3.8}$$

Because (3.7) and (3.8) are considered to be conditions rarely satisfied, it is assumed that (3.6) is almost always negative.

3.4 A problem-shift in the Hicks–Allen Programme

1. Part I of Hicks's *Value and Capital* (1939) is generally recognized to contain a restatement of the problem of revising Marshall's theory of consumer behaviour and the ordinalist solution of Hicks and Allen, as well as an integration of ordinal utility theory into a general theory of price determination. However, it has gone unnoticed in the literature that Hicks's restatement of the problem is substantially different from the original formulation of Hicks and Allen (1934). This point escaped the attention of such influential commentators as Schumpeter (1954, pt IV, appendix to ch. 7), Houthakker (1961) and Shackle (1967, ch. 8), as well as reviewers of *Value and Capital* (see Harrod, 1939; Haley, 1939; Boulding, 1939; Machlup, 1940; and Morgenstern, 1941). This change, or problem-shift,[6] as we shall argue greatly diminishes the importance that has been attached to the Hicks–Allen Programme.

2. It should be remembered that, for Hicks and Allen, the acceptance of Pareto's proof of the immeasurability of utility required the rejection of Marshall's theory. It was in this context that the problem of how to revise Marshall's theory arose (Hicks and Allen, 1934, p. 55, emphasis added):

> What has now to be done is to take in turn a number of the main concepts which have been evolved by the subjective theory; *to examine which of them are affected by the immeasurability of utility; and of those which have to be abandoned,* to enquire what, if anything, can be put in their place. It is hoped in this way to assist in the construction of a theory of value in which all concepts that pretend to quantitative exactitude, can be rigidly and exactly defined.

The major ingredient of their solution is the concept of a scale of preferences, or ordinal utility. The change from a cardinal to an ordinal concept of utility, in Hicks's and Allen's opinion, 'rested on a positive demonstration that *the facts of observable conduct make a scale of preferences capable of theoretical construction* . . . but they do not enable us to proceed from the scale of preference to a particular utility function' (1934, p. 52; emphasis added).

3. In Hicks (1939) the rationale for revising Marshall's theory is changed. The revision is not defended on the grounds that an ordinal utility rather than a cardinal utility function can be constructed from the facts of observable conduct, but on the grounds that only an ordinal concept of utility is necessary for the explanation of consumer behaviour (p. 18, emphasis added):

> Pareto's discovery only opens a door, which we can enter *or* not as we feel inclined. But from the technical economic point of view there are strong reasons for supposing we ought to enter it. The quantitative concept of utility is *not necessary* in order to explain market phenomena. Therefore, on the principle of Occam's razor, it is better to do without it.

4. The citing of 'Occam's razor' reveals a change in Hicks's attitude to the question whether utility, cardinal or ordinal, is an observational concept. This is evident from the fact that the reference to Pareto's discovery in the above passage is not to his proof of immeasurability of utility but to his innovative use of indifference maps (Hicks, 1939, p. 16, emphasis added):

> We come now to the really remarkable thing about *indifference curves – the discovery* which shunted Pareto's theory on to a different line from Marshall's, and opened a way to new results of wide economic significance.

Moreover, nowhere in *Value and Capital* does Hicks assert that the 'facts of observable conduct' enable, theoretically, a scale of preferences (an ordinal utility function) to be constructed. Pareto's proof of the immeasurability of utility, which is Hicks's and Allen's *raison d'être* for revising Marshall's theory, goes unmentioned in *Value and Capital*.

5. In arguing that only an ordinal concept of utility is necessary to explain consumer behaviour, Hicks drops two important situational constraints from the Hicks–Allen problem of revising Marshall's theory, namely that concepts should correspond to observable phenomena and that utility is not measurable. It is not suggested here that Hicks replaced these two constraints by their converse. The point is simply that the issue of measurability of utility and the wider issue that concepts should be observational are irrelevant and immaterial to Hicks's reformulation of the problem. Although Hicks himself prefers an ordinal concept of

utility, he does adopt a more tolerant attitude towards those who subscribe to a cardinal concept (1939, p. 18):

> Now of course this does not mean that if any one has any other ground for supposing that there exists some suitable quantitative measure of utility, or satisfaction, or desiredness, there is anything in the above argument to set against it. If one is a utilitarian in philosophy, one has a perfect right to be a utilitarian in one's economics. But if one is not (and few people are utilitarians nowadays), one also has the right to an economics free of utilitarian assumptions.

6. Unfortunately, it is this tolerance that undermines the significance of the Hicks–Allen problem. Since it is now Hicks's opinion that the belief in measurability is not unreasonable, as it was considered in Hicks and Allen (1934), it cannot be argued that there is the same sense of urgency in revising Marshall's theory.[7] Consequently, the significance of the Hicks–Allen Programme in the theory of consumer behaviour needs to be reconsidered.[8]

7. It must now be asked why Hicks changes his attitude to Pareto's proof, and drops, in the process, the two situational constraints to which the Hicks–Allen theory owes its importance. Hicks himself does not mention, and neither does he allude to, the fact that emphasis has shifted from Pareto's proof to the latter's innovative use of indifference maps. The task for us here is to set out the logic of a continual acceptance in the Hicks–Allen Programme of Pareto's claim that a scale of preferences, but not a cardinal utility function, can be constructed from the facts of observable conduct.

8. We conjecture that Hicks abandons his previous position because he appreciates the difficulties that are associated with any actual attempt to construct indifference maps.

9. Consider, for example, the method of constructing an individual's indifference map through questioning him. In the context of the Hicks–Allen Programme, this procedure is unacceptable because it does not use facts of observable conduct. If this procedure were acceptable, their objection to measurable utility would vanish, for if it is permissible to question an individual about the scale of his preferences, there can be no valid objection against questioning him about the intensity of his preferences. There remains, however, the question whether a consumer knows his preferences, the scale and/or intensity of them.

10. The only viable alternative from the Hicks–Allen position is to draw on observations of an individual's market behaviour. But this procedure encounters a serious difficulty. If observations of market behaviour are used to construct a scale of preferences, it turns ordinal utility theory into a circular explanation of consumer behaviour: consumer market behaviour is explained in terms of the individual's scale of preferences, or ordinal utility function, which, in turn, is explained by his market behaviour.[9]

11. There is another difficulty. It may be impossible to discern an individual's preferences from observations of his market behaviour if these preferences are influenced by the material circumstances, i.e. prices and income. This point is evident from Hicks's comment on the applicability of his analysis of consumer behaviour to other fields (1939, p. 55):

> The objects bought and sold need not be consumers' goods, or they need not all be consumers' goods; the necessary condition is only that they should be objects of desire, which can be bought and sold, and which can be arranged in an order of preferences (an indifference system) *which is itself independent of prices.*

3.5 On the law of diminishing marginal rate of substitution

1. If the concepts of utility and marginal utility are replaced, then so must the law of diminishing marginal utility be replaced. Hicks (1939) argues that a replacement for this law is necessary to ensure that the point of equilibrium is stable. To serve this end, the law (principle) of diminishing marginal rate of substitution[10] is proposed: the more of good x_1 that is substituted for good x_2, such that the consumer maintains his level of satisfaction, the less will be the amount of x_2 given up for successive amounts of x_1.

2. In this section we will examine the reason that is given as to why the law of diminishing marginal rate of substitution (LDMRS) is necessary for the Hicks–Allen theory. With reference to the explanation given in Hicks (1939), we shall argue that the theoretical necessity of the LDMRS should be distinguished from the issue of whether the LDMRS is true or not, and that these two issues are confused in the Hicks–Allen theory.

3. The theoretical necessity of the LDMRS is stated in Hicks (1939) as the requirement that the point of equilibrium should be

stable. This is incorrect because Hicks stipulates that a condition for a point to be an equilibrium one is that it must be stable. The necessity of the law for the Hicks–Allen explanation of consumer behaviour can be briefly stated as follows. In order to explain why a particular bundle, X^0, is bought, it is insufficient to say that X^0 is the bundle which maximizes the consumer's satisfaction. In more positive terms, it is necessary to explain why all other bundles other than X^0 were not bought. That is why the budget constraint alone is regarded as an unsatisfactory explanation because it rules out from consideration only those bundles which exceed the value of the budget. An explanation is still needed as to why bundles which cost less than or are equal to the budget are not bought. It is in the context of this problem in the theory of consumer behaviour that the issue of stability arises.

4. Consider, for example, Figure 3.1, in which the preferences of a consumer are represented by indifference curves which contain 'flat' portions. With the given budget, the point of maximum utility is not unique. In other words, the statement that X^0 was bought because it is the point of maximum utility is an unsatisfactory answer to the question of why X^0 was bought by the consumer since all bundles between X^1 and X^n are points of (equi-) maximum

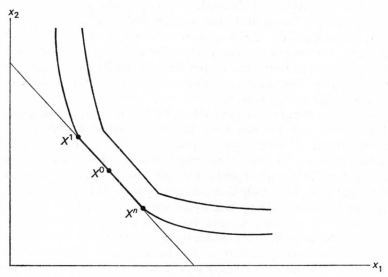

Figure 3.1

utility. A satisfactory answer would require in addition an explanation of why all bundles other than X^0 were not bought. Instead of introducing additional premises to complete the explanation, the Hicks–Allen theory rules out explicitly the possibility of multiple equilibria[11] through the requirement that the law of diminishing marginal rate of substitution is true.

5. Therefore, by requiring that the marginal rate of substitution be diminishing everywhere, any point of maximum utility is unique for some given budget. In terms of the logic of explanation, it is a logically satisfactory explanation to say that a consumer bought what he did because it is the bundle which gives him the maximum utility in the given material circumstances.

6. While it is not difficult to appreciate the importance of the law for the explanation of consumer behaviour, the question of whether the law is true or not still remains. For even if the law enables Hicks to give a logically satisfactory explanation of consumer behaviour, the empirical falsity of the law implies that the explanation is false. In Marshall's theory, the law of diminishing marginal utility, which is the analogous requirement for a complete explanation, was held to be a universal truth of human nature; its truth was considered to be intuitively obvious. Although Hicks makes no such appeal to intuition for the law of diminishing marginal rate of substitution, he nevertheless feels that the law requires justification.

7. Hicks seeks the justification by reflecting on the purpose that the law is to serve in the theory. However, the purpose of the law is a separate issue from that of the truth or falsity of the law. By confusing two separate issues, he makes the issue of truth subsidiary to that of theoretical necessity.

8. The justification for the truth of the law is given in two parts. First, Hicks explains why there are some cases of a diminishing marginal rate of substitution, to paraphrase Hicks, why the law is sometimes true, i.e. why some marginal rates of substitution are diminishing. Then he explains why the law is true, i.e. why all marginal rates of substitution are diminishing. Hicks regards the first explanation as the prelude to the second.

9. The law is sometimes true, according to Hicks, because for a point to be an equilibrium point, the marginal rate of substitution must be diminishing at that point. The next question then is 'Do equilibrium points exist?' Hicks says 'Yes.' His reason is that 'some points of possible equilibrium do exist on the indifference maps of

nearly every one (that is to say, they do decide to buy such-and-such quantities of commodities, and do not stay hesitating indefinitely like Buridan's ass)' (1939, p. 22). In other words, equilibrium points exist because people do buy. But how can Hicks equate the existence of equilibrium points with the fact that people do buy?

10. The link between the existence of equilibrium and the fact that people do buy is the implicit assumption that people always buy the bundle that maximizes their satisfaction, given the material circumstances of price and income. Thus to assert the existence of equilibrium points is equivalent to the assertion that the Hicks–Allen theory of consumer behaviour is true.

11. Hicks correctly points out that the law must be more than sometimes true if it is to be of any use in economic theory. The interest is not only in the explanation of a single act of consumption but in all acts of consumption: 'It is clear, therefore, that for any point to be a possible rate of equilibrium at appropriate prices the marginal rate of substitution at that point must be diminishing' (Hicks, 1939, p. 22). When the market conditions, i.e. prices and/or income, change, Hicks wants to be able to explain why the consumer buys a different bundle (1939, p. 23):

> When market conditions change, the consumer moves from one point of equilibrium to another point of equilibrium; at each of these positions the condition of diminishing marginal rate of substitution holds, or he could not take up such a position at all.

It is clear, then, that the law is needed to ensure the completeness of the explanation of consumer behaviour. Moreover, the law is needed in order 'to deduce from it laws of market conduct – laws, that is, which deal with the reaction of the consumer to changes in market conditions' (Hicks, 1939, p. 23). These laws explain the direction and magnitude of change in the quantity bought when the material circumstances confronting the consumer change.

12. Hicks says that when market conditions change, the consumer moves from one position of equilibrium to another, i.e. he buys a different bundle when the prices and income change. But why should the consumer buy a different bundle when market conditions change? Hicks does not say. Because Hicks requires that for a bundle to be bought, i.e. to be an equilibrium point, the marginal rate of substitution must be diminishing; a new bundle will necessarily be bought when market conditions change.

13. For the marginal rate of substitution to be diminishing every-where, Hicks assumes that between any two positions of equilibrium, all positions must exhibit a diminishing marginal rate of substitution, i.e. there are no 'kinks' in the curves between two equilibrium points. If there are such perversities, Hicks observes that 'curious con-sequences follow, such that there will be some systems of prices at which *the consumer will be unable to choose* between two different ways of spending his income' (1939, p. 23; emphasis added). This suggests that the assumption guarantees that a consumer can act decisively in accordance with the theory. If a consumer wants to act in accordance with the principle that he should maximize his utility subject to material circumstances, this assumption of regularity ensures that there will be one and only one bundle which will maximize his utility in any given material circumstances. However, the theory is not concerned with whether a consumer can act in accordance with the theory but whether he does act in accordance with it – that his actions can be explained by the theory.

14. To appreciate why Hicks assumes the truth of the law, we must consider why Hicks is interested in the intermediate points between equilibrium points. Hicks is concerned with intermediate points because he wants to make explicable whatever bundle is bought by a consumer. If the marginal rate of substitution is not diminishing at the intermediate points, there is the possibility of multiple equilibria, i.e. there is more than one bundle which maxi-mizes utility subject to the given material conditions (Hicks and Allen, 1934, p. 58):

> The assumption that the principle of increasing [diminishing] marginal rate of substitution is universally true, thus means simply that any point, throughout the region we are considering, might be a point of equilibrium with appropriate prices.

15. Therefore, 'kinks' are ruled out by assumption, not because their existence implies that a consumer is unable to choose between two or more bundles but because Hicks wants to explain why a con-sumer bought a particular bundle rather than some other. Hicks wishes us to believe that if there are 'kinks' the consumer is not only unable to choose but will not choose. Clearly, the task for Hicks and for the theorist is to explain what the consumer chooses.[12]

16. In the beginning of this section, we drew attention to the fact that the logical necessity of the law is a separate question from the

empirical truth of the law. It is evident that Hicks confuses these two questions. For Hicks, the law is true because it is necessary for the theory. This implies that for Hicks the truth of the theory is beyond question. Although Hicks does say that the law's 'accordance with experience seems definitely good' (1939, p. 24), consider how he would react to counter-evidence to this law (Hicks and Allen, 1934, p. 58, emphasis added):

> There must be some points at which it is true, or we could get no equilibrium at all. To assume it true universally is a serious assumption but one which seems justifiable until significant facts are adduced which make it *necessary for us to pay careful attention to exceptions.*

While significant facts should prompt Hicks to reconsider both the law and the facts, Hicks will countenance reconsideration only of the facts. This flagrant disregard for the truth of the law underscores the fundamental importance of the law for the Hicks–Allen theory of consumer behaviour.

3.6 On the law of demand in the Hicks–Allen theory

1. In the history of the theory of consumer behaviour, the law of demand occupies a special place. At one time a theory of consumer behaviour was judged solely on its ability to explain the law.[13] In the 1970s, the opinion of specialists is divided.[14] However, throughout his writings on consumer theory, Hicks is unequivocal on his position (1956, p. 189):

> The prime concern of demand theory is with the Law of Demand. It is from the standpoint of its effect in elucidating the law of demand that our theory may best be summarized, and that it may claim to be judged.

2. Chapter 2 of Hicks's *Value and Capital* (1939) is entitled 'The Law of Consumer's Demand'. This underscores the significance of the law to the Hicks–Allen Programme of revising Marshall's theory. Because the law of demand is derivable in Marshall's theory, its derivation became a major theoretical task for the Hicks–Allen theory. We are therefore in agreement with Shackle's assessment (1967, p. 86) of the two theories:

> To give this 'law of demand' some reasoned position in our

store of ideas, to find other propositions which can be exhibited as the premises from which it flows or as consequences which flow from it, to build under it an explanatory argument; this sort of purpose is, for Marshall and Hicks alike, the central if not almost the sole concern of the theory of consumer's demand.

3. The fact that the law of demand is not derivable from the Hicks–Allen theory was seen by Hicks and Allen as a minor deficiency in their theory. They argued that upward-sloping demand curves, the exceptions to the law, are rare because they are examples of the pathological phenomenon of Giffen goods, which, in their opinion, are unlikely empirical occurrences. In the words of Hicks, 'the simple law of demand – the downward slope of the demand curve – turns out to be almost infallible in its workings' (1939, p. 35). In this section, we shall criticize this argument on the grounds that it is both *ad hoc* and insufficient to resolve the theoretical difficulty, namely the logical possibility of upward-sloping demand curves. In addition, we shall set out the alternative strategies that Hicks and Allen could have taken to deal with the theoretical difficulty.

4. It is important to note that Hicks and Allen thought it was necessary to deal with exceptions to the law. This view is not widely held. To many economists the logical possibility of upward-sloping demand curves in the Hicks–Allen theory remains a curiosity. Stigler is representative of this large body of opinion when he chides economists for devoting too much attention to this issue:[15]

> For more than half a century economists have recognized the possibility of a positively sloping demand curve. They have desired a real example, probably to reassure themselves of the need for discussing the possibility and almost invariably they have used Marshall's Giffen paradox as this example (1947, p. 152).

5. The possibility of deriving an upward-sloping demand curve in the Hicks–Allen theory is due to the unknown sign of the income term of the Slutsky equation for the change in quantity bought with respect to the change in its own price. That the substitution term is negative is a consequence of the law of diminishing marginal rate of substitution but the theory places no restriction on the sign of the income term. Thus there arises in the Hicks–Allen theory the unintended logical possibility of upward-sloping demand curves, the counter-examples to the law of demand.

6. Exceptions to the law of demand are identified by Hicks and Allen as examples of the Giffen case, and since they considered this phenomenon to be rare, they concluded that the law is almost infallible in its working:[16]

> it is only possible at low levels of income, when a large proportion of expenditure is devoted to this 'inferior' commodity, and when, among the small number of other objects consumed, there are none that are at all easily substitutable for the first. As the standard of living rises, and expenditure becomes increasingly diversified it is a situation which becomes increasingly improbable (1934, pp. 68–9).

Similarly, Hicks writes (1939, p. 35):

> Consumers are likely to spend a large proportion of their incomes upon what is for them an inferior good if their standard of living is very low. The famous Giffen case, quoted by Marshall, exactly fits these requirements. At a low level of income, consumers may satisfy the greater part of their need for food by one staple foodstuff (bread in the Giffen case), which will be replaced by a more varied diet if income rises. If the price of this staple falls, they have a quite considerable surplus available for expenditure, and they may spend this surplus upon more interesting foods, which then take the place of the staple, and reduce the demand for it. In such a case as this, the negative income effect may be strong enough to outweigh the substitution effect. But it is evident how rare such cases must be.

7. Before we determine whether the argument is sufficient to exclude the possibility of upward-sloping demand curves, we shall first comment on the validity of the method of argument.

8. In citing empirical evidence to resolve a theoretical difficulty, Hicks and Allen are confusing a question of fact with a question of logic (see section 3.5 above). An enquiry into the empirical existence of upward-sloping demand curves is of no relevance to the question, of whether or not the law of demand is derivable from the theory. It is apparent that the appeal to the facts is purely *ad hoc*. For example, Hicks and Allen do not cite any empirical evidence for the proposition that the substitution term is negative. Although this proposition is derivable from the theory, it is an open question

whether it is empirically true. Our contention that there is a deep-seated confusion of logic with fact is supported by a consideration of the reason given for the truth of the law: 'It follows that in strictness the Law of Demand is a hybrid; it has one leg resting in theory, and one in observation' (Hicks, 1956, p. 59). On this account it would be impossible to cite empirical evidence for or against the law of demand.

9. Let us now consider the validity of the Hicks–Allen argument that upward-sloping demand curves are rare because Giffen goods are rare.

10. We must first determine the necessary and sufficient conditions for an upward-sloping demand curve in the context of the Hicks–Allen theory. The Slutsky equation for the change in quantity bought of a good, x_i, with respect to a change in its price, p_i, is

$$(\delta x_i/\delta p_i) = (\delta x_i/\delta p_i)_{U=U_0} - x_i(\delta x_i/\delta I) \qquad (3.6)$$

because

$$x_i > 0, \qquad (\delta x_i/\delta p_i)_{U=U_0} < 0. \qquad (3.6^*)$$

(3.6) takes on a positive value if and only if x_i is an inferior good:

$$(\delta x_i/\delta I) < 0 \qquad (3.7)$$

and

$$\mid x_i(\delta x_i/\delta I) \mid > \mid (\delta x_i/\delta p_i)_{U=U_0} \mid. \qquad (3.8)$$

11. The characteristics of a Giffen good are identified by Hicks and Allen as follows:

(a) the good is inferior;
(b) the standard of living of the individual is low; and
(c) a large proportion of the individual's income is spent on that good.

While (a) is a necessary condition for an upward-sloping demand curve in the Hicks–Allen theory, it is obviously not sufficient. However, (b) and (c) are not equivalent to (3.8). The fact that a good with an upward-sloping demand curve is inferior does not necessarily mean that the individual concerned has a low standard of living and that he spends a large proportion of his income on that good. Within the context of the Hicks–Allen theory, there is no criteria for determining what is a low standard of living or what constitutes a large proportion of an individual's income. Given the conditions for an upward-sloping demand curve in the Hicks–Allen theory, it is clear that what matters is the relative size of the absolute values of the income and substitution terms. Thus, in the Hicks–Allen theory a Giffen good is not the same thing as a good with an upward-sloping demand curve.[17]

12. The error in Hicks's and Allen's argument can be attributed to their uncritical appropriation of Marshall's explanation of the Giffen good. Marshall (1920) argued that it is through the effect on the marginal utility of income that a rise in the price of a good upon which an individual spends a large proportion of his income can lead to a rise in the demand for the good.[18]

13. Thus we conclude that even if we disregard the illegitimacy of Hicks's and Allen's use of empirical evidence to resolve a theoretical difficulty, the argument is nevertheless insufficient to exclude the logical possibility of an upward-sloping demand curve.

14. What logical options remain to resolve the theoretical difficulty in the Hicks–Allen theory? First, the assumption that all goods are non-inferior can be added to the theory to exclude the logical possibility of upward-sloping demand curves. Second, the theory can be amended to exclude all inferior goods which give rise to upward-sloping demand curves. Third, the unintended logical consequence of upward-sloping demand curves can be reinterpreted as an intended logical consequence of the theory.[19] If any one of the three options are taken, consideration must be given to the implications of the change not only for the Hicks–Allen theory but also for the theory of price, of which the Hicks–Allen theory is an integral part.

Chapter 4

A new theory

4.1 The problem-situation of Samuelson (1938a)

1. In this chapter we propose a solution to the problem of understanding revealed preference theory as presented in Samuelson (1938a). Our solution is to show that for Samuelson the theory is a satisfactory solution to the problem of deriving the main results of ordinal utility theory without the use of utility or any other non-observational concept. This rational reconstruction of the problem-situation is presented in this section and the next. In section 4.3 we shall criticize Samuelson's solution on the grounds that it does not avoid the use of non-observational concepts and propositions. Finally, in section 4.4 we shall argue that Samuelson mis-specified the actual problem-situation by excluding the aim of explanation as an objective of ordinal utility theory. In addition, we shall demonstrate that an explanation of consumer behaviour cannot be constructed from Samuelson's theory.

2. Before we accept a replacement for an existing theory, we must satisfy ourselves that the new theory meets certain minimal requirements: first, we require that the new theory attains the theoretical aims of the existing theory; and second, that there are certain advantages of the new theory over the old one. Both are necessary conditions. Otherwise, we may have a situation where the new theory has certain advantages but does not attain the same aims or attains the same aims but does not possess any additional advantages.[1]

3. In proposing a new theory of consumer behaviour, Samuelson (1938a) demonstrated that his new theory, which we shall call the 'Samuelson Theory',[2] succeeded in achieving the theoretical aims of

ordinal utility theory. He identified these aims as the derivation of the following conditions: (1) the single-valuedness of demand functions; (2) the homogeneity of degree zero of demand functions; and (3) the negative semi-definiteness of the substitution matrix. There is, however, an advantage of the new theory, argued Samuelson: it avoids any reliance on the concept of utility or on any other concept which does not correspond to observable phenomena. Thus Samuelson offered a replacement for ordinal utility theory.

4. This interpretation of what Samuelson hoped to achieve through his new approach contradicts the interpretation that can be found in the literature. Most writers regard Samuelson (1938a) as an attempt to derive the necessary and sufficient observational conditions for ordinal utility theory and conclude that it succeeded only in discovering the necessary condition (see, for example, Houthakker,[3] 1950 and 1961; Gale, 1960; Uzawa, 1960; Richter, 1966; Georgescu-Roegen, 1968; Kihlstrom, Mas-Colell and Sonnenschein, 1976). Thus Gale (1960, p. 348) writes that 'Samuelson first enunciated the Weak Axiom which gives a necessary condition for the "rationality" of a consumer's behaviour.' By 'rationality', is meant behaviour that can be described as the outcome of consistent maximization of a utility function.

5. Therefore, it may be said that the new approach should not be considered as a new theory. However, there is strong textual evidence supporting our contention that Samuelson was interested in changing the fundamental ideas that economists held about consumer behaviour. For example, the problem of integrability, which is concerned with the construction of an individual's utility function from observations of his behaviour, was rejected by Samuelson as an unacceptable consideration within the context of the new framework (1938a, p. 68):

> I cannot see that it is really an important problem, particularly
> if we are willing to dispense with the utility concept and its
> vestigial remnants . . . I should strongly deny, however, that for
> a rational and consistent individual integrability is implied,
> except possibly as a matter of circular definition.

In the addendum to the original paper, he wrote: 'In the February issue of this journal I suggested that the theory of consumer's behaviour could be founded on three postulates' (1938b, p. 353). In a paper on the empirical implications of ordinal utility theory,[4] he reiterated (1938c, p. 346, emphasis added):

> Recently I proposed a *new* postulational base upon which to construct a theory of consumer's behavior. It was there shown that from this starting point could be erected a theory which included all the elements of the previous analysis.

If theories are differentiated by the fundamental assumptions made, then a new postulational base, in conjunction with an explicit rejection of ordinal utility theory, must be interpreted as a new theory of consumer behaviour. Thus we shall interpret the first paper (1938a) as a proposal for a new theory of consumer behaviour.

6. To understand why Samuelson thought it necessary to create a new theory of consumer behaviour, we must understand his objections to ordinal utility theory. In terms of the method of rational reconstruction, we must reconstruct his appraisal of ordinal utility theory. This appraisal is an important component of his (reconstructed) problem-situation, for it provides the justification for the creation of a new theory.

7. Samuelson's objections to ordinal utility theory are carried over from his objections to cardinal utility theory. He discarded cardinal utility theory thus (1938a, p. 61):

> The discrediting of *utility* as a psychological concept robbed it of its possible virtue as an *explanation* of human behaviour in other than a circular sense, revealing its emptiness as even a construction.

8. The break-up of utility theory, to which Samuelson alludes, is over the justification of its explanation of consumer behaviour.[5] It was asked of the theory: 'How do you know that a consumer is maximizing utility when you observe him buying a particular combination of goods?' The reply was that the explanation is unquestionably true if we only reflect a little on our everyday experience. In the now famous *Essay on the Nature and Significance of Economic Science*, Lionel Robbins articulated this appeal for introspection. The postulates of economics 'are so much the stuff of our everyday experience that they have only to be stated to be recognised as obvious' (1935, p. 79; see also p. 105).

9. Another route for the justification of the truth of utility theory was taken by some Austrian economists (see Sweezy, 1934, p. 178).

They argued that the theory is true because in maximizing utility or satisfaction, an individual is engaging in behaviour that is proper from an economic point of view. This is reasoning in a circular fashion because proper behaviour from an economic point of view is taken to mean acting so as to maximize utility.

10. Although Samuelson did not say so, it appears that he would reject both lines of reasoning as unscientific, since in his opinion only an inter-subjectively observable process may be used to justify a theory.

11. In Samuelson's opinion, the ordinalist revision of utility theory by Hicks and Allen moved in the right direction, but it failed to sever all links with the discredited concept of utility. Vestigial traces remained (1938a, p. 62):

> The introduction and meaning of the marginal rate of
> substitution as an entity independent of any psychological,
> introspective implications would be, to say the least, ambiguous,
> and would seem an artificial convention in the explanation of
> price behavior.

Consider, for example, the law of diminishing marginal rate of substitution (LDMRS), which replaced the law of diminishing marginal utility. Samuelson (1938a, p. 61) asked why one should believe in the LDMRS. A justification by introspection is clearly unacceptable. Also, it is logically invalid to argue that the LDMRS is true because it leads to plausible demand curves. Furthermore, as Samuelson (1938a, p. 61) pointed out, the argument is circular because it is sometimes advanced that these curves are plausible because they follow from the LDMRS. For Samuelson the want of demonstration is evident enough.

12. Samuelson's appraisal of utility theory and its ordinalist revision can be summarized as follows. Both versions are unacceptable because they are based on non-observational concepts and propositions which are not justifiable in terms of observations.

13. How, then, should theories be justified? It is clear that for Samuelson justification must come from observations of actual behaviour. Instead of demonstrating the truth of ordinal utility theory from observations, which, for Samuelson, is an artificial way of proceeding, he called for the creation of a theory that is expressed directly in observational terms (1938a, p. 62, emphasis added):

> I propose, therefore, that we start anew in direct attack upon

49

the problem, dropping off the last vestiges of the utility analysis. This does not preclude the introduction of utility by any who may care to do so, nor will it contradict the results attained by the use of related constructs. *It is merely that the analysis can be carried on more directly, and from a different set of postulates.*

Furthermore, in the conclusion to the first paper (1938a), Samuelson wrote: 'It is hoped, however, that the orientation given here is more directly based upon those elements which must be taken as *data* by economic science, and is more meaningful in its formulation' (pp. 70–1).

14. It should be noted that Samuelson's interpretation of ordinal utility theory had already been rejected by Hicks and Allen. Following Pareto, they held that an indifference map or a scale of preferences is 'capable of theoretical construction' (1934, p. 52) from facts of observable conduct. The indifference map is the main component of their solution to the problem of revising Marshall's theory without the use of an immeasurable concept of utility. It seems that the issue that divides Hicks–Allen and Samuelson is over what constitutes observations of actual behaviour. While Hicks and Allen would admit experimental as well as market observations, Samuelson would accept only market observations.[6]

15. In Samuelson's appraisal of utility theory, we can discern two important situational constraints in his problem-situation. First, Samuelson accepts the view that all knowledge must be provable, demonstrable, or justifiable. It is from this epistemological position that he insists on the justification of the theories.[7] In fact, it forms the basis for his rejection of utility and its ordinalist version. Second, he requires that proof or demonstration must be from observations and that these observations are of market behaviour. Observation, in his opinion, is the most secure source of knowledge. These philosophical views gave Samuelson sufficient reasons for rejecting the previous theory, and thus for creating a new theory. Neither utility theory nor its ordinalist revision, in Samuelson's opinion, meet these criteria.

16. Although the two philosophical constraints are sufficient reasons for creating a new theory, they do not require Samuelson to do so. Another option is open. He could have tried to reformulate the non-observational ordinal utility theory in terms of observational concepts. But Samuelson (1938a, p. 62) dismissed this course of

action as an indirect and roundabout way of proceeding. (Surprisingly, we shall find in Samuelson (1948) the presumption that this latter option was, in fact, taken and that this is the proper interpretation of Samuelson (1938a).)

17. It should be pointed out that Samuelson's main objection to the Hicks–Allen theory is meta-theoretical, as was Hicks's and Allen's objection to Marshall's theory. In each case the new theory was created not because it explained some situations that were unexplained by the previous theory but, rather, the previous theory was discarded because it failed from a methodological standpoint, i.e. it used non-observational concepts.

18. In summary, the problem-situation of Samuelson (1938a) is to derive the main results of ordinal utility theory without the use of utility or any other non-observational concept. This problem arose for Samuelson because utility theory and its ordinalist revision were not justifiable in terms of market observations.

4.2 The Samuelson solution

1. The main feature of the Samuelson Theory is a postulate of consistency of behaviour which later became known as the 'weak axiom of revealed preference'. It is stated in formal terms as follows:

For all pairs of bundles, X^0, X^1, if
$X^0 \Phi X^1$ then not $(X^1 \Phi X^0)$ where
$X^0 \Phi X^1 =_{df} P^0 X^0 \geq P^0 X^1$ and X^0 is bought at
price–income situation (P^0, I^0).

This postulate, which we shall call the 'Samuelson Postulate',[8] means that 'if an individual selects batch one over batch two, he does not at the same time select two over one' (Samuelson, 1938a, p. 65). According to Samuelson its meaning is 'perfectly clear and will probably gain ready acquiescence' (1938a, p. 65).

2. In Samuelson (1938a, 1938b) it is shown that from the Samuelson Postulate, in conjunction with the assumptions that demand functions are given and that all income is spent, the major results of ordinal utility theory can be derived:

(1) the single-valuedness of demand functions;
(2) the homogeneity of degree zero of demand functions; and
(3) the negative semi-definiteness of the substitution matrix.[9]

3. In Samuelson's opinion, the Samuelson Theory satisfies the

epistemological/methodological requirement that it must be justifiable in terms of market observations. The Samuelson Postulate and its auxiliary propositions are expressed in observational terms (prices, quantities and income) which correspond to observable entities: 'the orientation given here is more directly based upon those elements which must be taken as *data* by economic science' (Samuelson, 1938a, p. 71). The theory becomes amenable to empirical verification. Thus we can understand why Samuelson considers that his theory is a satisfactory solution to the problem of deriving the main results of ordinal utility theory (OUT) without the use of non-observational concepts.

4. Following closely the presentation in Samuelson (1938a, 1938b), we now derive the three major results of OUT from the Samuelson Theory, the major proposition of which is the Samuelson Postulate.

5. First, we give the derivation of the negative semi-definite substitution matrix. Assume that the demand functions of the consumer are known, that is to say, for a given set of prices and a given income, we know the amounts of each good that the consumer purchases (or will purchase) and that the demand functions can be differentiated. These demand functions are said to be observational because all its terms – prices, quantities and income – correspond to observable entities. Suppose

$$[X^1P^0 = X^0P^0], \tag{4.1}$$

which implies by the Samuelson Postulate that

$$[X^0P^1 > X^1P^1]. \tag{4.2}$$

Rewrite (4.1) and (4.2) as

$$[(X^0 + \Delta X)P^0] = [X^0P^0] \tag{4.3}$$

and

$$[X^0 (P^0 + \Delta P)] > [(X^0 + \Delta X) (P^0 + \Delta P)]. \tag{4.4}$$

Rewrite (4.3) and (4.4) in limiting form, dropping the square brackets and the superscripts:

$$\sum_{i=1}^{n} p_i dx_i = 0 \tag{4.5}$$

$$\sum_{i=1}^{n} dp_i dx_i < 0 \tag{4.6}$$

not all dx_i or $dp_i = 0$.

Given demand functions that can be differentiated, each of the form $x_i = h^i(P_1, \ldots, p_n, I)$, for all $i = 1, \ldots, n$, then

$$dx_i = \Sigma h_j dp_j + h_I^i dI, \qquad i = 1, \ldots, n \tag{4.7}$$

$$dI = \Sigma x_j dp_j + \Sigma p_j dx_j. \tag{4.8}$$

From (4.5), (4.8) becomes

$$dI = \Sigma x_j dp_j. \tag{4.9}$$

Rewrite (4.7) as

$$dx_i = \Sigma h_j dp_j + h \; \Sigma x_j dp_j = \Sigma(h \; + h \; x_j) dp_j. \tag{4.10}$$

Then (4.6) becomes

$$\Sigma\Sigma(h_j^i + h_I^i x_j) dp_i dp_j \leq 0. \tag{4.11}$$

Since $(h_j^i + h_I^i x_j) \neq (h \; + h_I^j x_i)$, because integrability is not assumed, define

$$K_{ij} = \frac{(h_j^i + h_I^i x_j) + (h_i^j + h_I^j x_i)}{2} = K_{ji}. \tag{4.12}$$

Then (4.11) becomes

$$\sum_{i=1}^{n} \; \sum_{j=1}^{n} \; (K_{ij}) dp_i dp_j \leq 0. \tag{4.13}$$

(4.12) is a negative semi-definite quadratic since for proportionate changes in prices it vanishes. From (4.12) we know that the $(n-1)$ principal minors alternate in sign, beginning with negative:

$$\left| K_{11} \right| < 0, \quad \begin{vmatrix} K_{11} & K_{12} \\ K_{21} & K_{22} \end{vmatrix} > 0, \text{ etc.,} \tag{4.14}$$

where

$$K = L \begin{vmatrix} K_{11}K_{12} \ldots K_{1n} \\ \cdot \\ \cdot \\ \cdot \\ \cdot \\ \cdot \\ K_{n1} \qquad K_{nn} \end{vmatrix}$$

which gives

$$(\delta x_i/\delta p_i + x_i \, \delta x_i/\delta I) < 0, \qquad i = i, \ldots, n \qquad (4.15)$$

$$(\delta x_i/\delta p_i + x_i \delta x_i/\delta I)(\delta x_j/\delta p_j + x_j \delta x_j/\delta I) - \{[(\delta x_i/\delta p_j + x_j \delta x_i/\delta I) + \delta x_j/\delta p_i + x_i \delta x_j/\delta I]/2\}^2 > 0; \qquad i,j = 1, \ldots, n, \, i \neq j; \text{ etc.}$$
$$(4.16)$$

(4.15) is commonly known as the Slutsky or substitution term, i.e. the residual variability of the ith good for a compensated change in the ith price. It can be written in the more familiar form, the Slutsky equation:

$$(\delta x_i/\delta p_i)_{U=U_0} = (\delta x_i/\delta p_i) + x_i(\delta x_i/\delta I),$$

or

$$(\delta x_i/\delta p_i) = (\delta x_i/\delta p_i)_{U=U_0} - x_i(\delta x_i/\delta I). \qquad (4.17)$$

6. To derive the homogeneity condition, i.e. that proportional changes in all prices and income leave the quantities demanded by the consumer unchanged, let $(p_1^0, \ldots, p_n^0, I^0)$ be the initial price–income situation and let $(x_1^0, \ldots, x_n^0)$ be the bundle bought in that situation. Let the second price–income situation be $(mp_1^0, \ldots, mp_n^0, mI^0)$, which is '$m$' times the initial price–income set, and let $(x_1^1, \ldots, x_n^1)$ be the bundle bought at the second situation. It needs to be shown that $x_i^1 = x_i^0$ for all $i = 1, \ldots, n$.

7. By definition:

$$I^1 = mI^0 \qquad (4.18)$$

$$\Sigma p_i^1 x_i^1 = m\Sigma p_i^0 x_i^0 \qquad (4.19)$$

$$p_i^1 = mp_i^0; \qquad i = 1, \ldots, n \qquad (4.20)$$

$$\Sigma p_i^0 x_i^1 = \Sigma p_i^0 x_i^0 \qquad (4.21)$$

$$\Sigma p_i^1 x_i^0 = \Sigma p_i^1 x_i^1 \qquad (4.22)$$

which contradicts the Samuelson Postulate since

$$\Sigma p^0 x_i^1 = \Sigma p_i^0 x_i^0 \text{ implies } \Sigma p_i^1 x_i^0 > \Sigma p_i^1 x_i^1. \qquad (4.23)$$

Hence $x_i^1 = x_i^0$ for all $i = 1, \ldots, n$.

8. To derive the single-valuedness of demand functions, use the previous analysis setting $m = 1$. Single-valuedness in the context of the theory means that when 'confronted with a given set of prices and with a given income, our idealised individual will always choose the same set of goods' (Samuelson, 1938a, p. 63).

9. It should be noted that in the derivation of the single-valuedness condition it is assumed that all income is spent. If all income is not spent, then it is possible for the Samuelson Postulate to be violated.

Suppose X^0 is bought at (P^0, I^0) and X^1 at (P^1, I^0), where $P^0 = P^1$. If not all income is spent when X^1 is bought, we have $P^0X^0 > P^0X^1$ and $P^1X^0 > P^1X^1$, which contradicts the Samuelson Postulate.

10. Together, the single-valuedness and homogeneity conditions are interpreted to mean that 'there will be a unique reaction to a given price and income situation' (Samuelson, 1938a, p. 63). In other words, whenever faced with a given price–income situation, the consumer buys the same bundle of goods.

11. The derivation of the single-valuedness and homogeneity of degree zero of demand functions and the negative semi-definiteness of the substitution matrix from the Samuelson Theory is regarded by Samuelson to be a satisfactory solution to his problem of deriving the main results of ordinal utility theory without the use of non-observational concepts. The Samuelson Theory is considered satisfactory because its major propositions contain only observational terms; that is to say, the Samuelson Postulate, the assumption of given demand functions and the assumption that all income is spent in each buying situation are verifiable empirically in terms of observations of market behaviour.

12. To summarize, our solution to the problem of understanding revealed preference theory (Samuelson Theory) as presented in Samuelson (1938a, 1938b) is the conjecture that the Samuelson Theory is a solution to the problem of deriving the main results of ordinal utility theory without the use of utility or any other non-observational concept and the explanation that, in Samuelson's opinion, the solution is satisfactory.

4.3 On the justification of the Samuelson Theory

1. In this section we are going to enquire into the acceptability of the Samuelson Theory as a solution to the problem of deriving the main results of ordinal utility theory without the use of the concept of utility or any other non-observational concept. We are particularly interested in determining whether or not the Samuelson Theory satisfies the epistemological/methodological constraints of the problem-situation, which, it should be remembered, provided Samuelson with sufficient reason for rejecting ordinal utility theory:

(1)   knowledge (theories) must be justifiable; and

(2)   justification must be from observations of market behaviour.

The outcome of this enquiry is internal criticism, while external criticism would be, for example, criticism of the demand for justification of knowledge, a consideration which is beyond the scope of this study.[10]

2. It is amply clear that Samuelson demanded a justification for accepting ordinal utility theory, asking: 'Why should one believe in the *increasing rate of marginal substitution*?' (1938a, p. 61). Accordingly, it can quite properly be asked of the Samuelson Theory: Why should one believe in the Samuelson Postulate? Our enquiry is facilitated by this focus on the Samuelson Postulate, for therein lies the theoretical innovation of the Samuelson Theory. If we conclude that the postulate is not verifiable empirically, the Samuelson Theory is ineligible as a replacement for ordinal utility theory and therefore cannot be a solution to Samuelson's problem of how to derive the three main results of ordinal utility theory without the use of non-observational concepts and propositions. In brief, we are evaluating Samuelson's reasons for declaring that this postulate of consistency of behaviour 'is perfectly clear and will gain ready acquiescence' (1938a, p. 65; see also p. 71).

3. At the outset we require a clarification of the interpretation assigned by Samuelson to the postulate. According to Samuelson, the postulate means 'that if an individual selects batch one over batch two, he does not *at the same time* select two over one' (1938a, p. 65; emphasis added). If this interpretation is what Samuelson intended, the postulate will, without doubt, gain ready acceptance because it is tautologically true: one cannot select both batches at the same time. The postulate needs no justification in terms of market observations or anything else. Surely, Samuelson did not intend this trivial interpretation of the postulate.[11]

4. The intended interpretation, it seems, is to define the postulate over two points of time: if an individual selects one batch when another batch does not cost more, then he cannot afford the first batch when he selects the second, where 'selects' means 'buys'. Given the interpretation of the postulate as a hypothesis, we can now pose the question: Why should one believe in the Samuelson Postulate?

5. Several possibilities come to mind as to how to justify the postulate. But for Samuelson the justification must come from observations of market behaviour, so we shall examine this first.

6. The Samuelson Postulate, it is said, is amenable to direct empirical verification because it is expressed solely in the observational terms of prices and quantities. But can the postulate be

justified by observations of market choices? The answer is 'No'. The domain of application of the postulate is defined over all market-choice situations (under perfect competition) of an individual. We can test the postulate against a finite number of possibilities, but there are an infinite number of market-choice situations, those that have been observed and those that have not. The postulate cannot therefore be verified empirically by observations of market choices.[12] Even if for a given number of market-choice situations the postulate is not falsified, there is no guarantee that it will not be falsified in some future market-choice situation, whether in a recurrence of an already observed price–income situation or the appearance of a new one. The truth of the postulate is not demonstrable; at best, we can only conjecture that it is true. However, to conjecture that the postulate holds for all possible market-choice situations would be inconsistent for Samuelson since that presumption is not justifiable from market observations.[13]

7. It may be argued that the Samuelson Postulate is justified because the three major results of ordinal utility theory can be derived from it (in conjunction with certain auxiliary hypotheses). This, however, implies that there is nothing novel about the Samuelson Theory. On what basis, then, can Samuelson call for the replacement of ordinal utility theory with his new theory if no advantage follows from so doing? Moreover, if Samuelson's sole interest is, in fact, in the derivation of these results, assuming them would suffice; every statement implies itself.[14] It should be remembered that Samuelson was interested not only in the derivation of these results but in their derivation from a set of statements which satisfy the epistemological/methodological constraints of his problem-situation. Therefore, to justify the Samuelson Postulate on the grounds that the three results can be derived is to abandon the claim for the methodological superiority of the new approach.

8. It is sometimes suggested that the Samuelson Theory is a simpler method by which the main results of ordinal utility theory can be derived (see, for example, Newman, 1965, pp. 130–1). But what is meant by 'simpler' is unclear. Is the Samuelson Theory simpler because it uses fewer assumptions ('Occam's razor'), because it is more susceptible to empirical verification or refutation, or because it is psychologically more appealing? Moreover, each of these interpretations of the concept of 'simplicity' is problematic (see Popper, 1935, ch. 7; and Schlesinger, 1963, ch. 1). Until the

principle of simplicity is more fully articulated by economists, the justification of the Samuelson Theory on the basis of simplicity would be unwarranted.

9. An appeal to introspection cannot be made, for the rejection of introspection formed a major part of Samuelson's criticism of ordinal utility theory (see Samuelson, 1938a, p. 61; and section 4.1 above).

10. On what basis, then, can Samuelson argue that his postulate will gain ready acceptance? Ready acceptance, we conjecture, comes from those who have already accepted ordinal utility theory.

11. Consider the following account of the market behaviour of an individual:

John bought X^0 at prices P^0 and spent his entire income I^0
At (P^0, I^0) the bundle X^1 did not cost more (A)
John bought X^1 at prices P^1 and spent his entire income I^1
At (P^1, I^1) the bundle X^0 did not cost more (B)

This behaviour, which is illustrated in Figure 4.1(a), is interpreted in the Samuelson Theory as inconsistent. Recall that the Samuelson Postulate is a postulate of consistency of behaviour, and, therefore, behaviour which 'violates' it is deemed inconsistent. But why should this behaviour be called 'inconsistent'? Is it not that the statement 'behaviour is inconsistent' is an abbreviated form of the statement 'behaviour is inconsistent *with respect to a given criterion*'? This point of view is supported by the interpretation that Samuelson assigns to the statement 'X^0 is selected over X^1'. It is a convenient abbreviation, for 'the individual could have purchased the second batch of goods with the price[s] and income of the first, *but did not choose to do so*' (Samuelson, 1938a, p. 65; emphasis added). To say that the individual 'did not choose to do so' is to presume that the consumer has a choice criterion.

12. The criterion to which the postulate appeals is that the first bundle cannot both be on a higher indifference curve and on a lower indifference curve than a second bundle (see Figure 4.1(b)). In other words, it is asserted that preferences are asymmetric. Thus, on the assumptions that preferences are asymmetric and that the individual buys according to his preferences, behaviour which 'violates' the Samuelson Postulate, such as that described by (A) and (B) above, can be interpreted as 'inconsistent'. As Sen correctly observed, this is tantamount to assuming the truth of ordinal utility theory:[15]

Faith in the axioms of revealed preference arises, therefore, not from empirical verification but from the intuitive reasonableness of these axioms interpreted precisely in terms of preference . . . if the theory of revealed preferences makes sense it does so not because no psychological assumptions are used but because the psychological assumptions used are sensibly chosen (1973, pp. 3–4).

From this assessment, Sen, unfortunately, does not turn to the question 'What problem does the Samuelson Theory (revealed preference theory) solve which is not solved by ordinal utility theory?'[16]

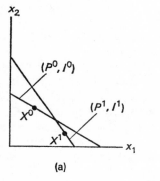 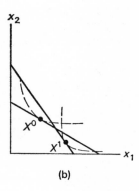

(a) (b)

Figure 4.1

13. The use of indifference curves is obviously illegitimate within a framework which aims to dispense with vestigial remnants of the utility concept, though it is a common practice in the literature, for example in Richter (1966, p. 639). Even in the original paper Samuelson slips into defending his new approach with ordinal utility theory: 'Woe to any who deny any one of the three postulates here! For they are, of course, deducible as theorems from the conventional analysis' (1938a, p. 70).

14. We hasten to point out that we have given an explanation of why Samuelson thought the postulate would gain ready acceptance by his fellow economists; it must not be interpreted as a proof that Samuelson justified his postulate in terms of an antecedent acceptance of ordinal utility theory, or that the Samuelson Theory can only be justified in this manner.

15. In the light of these remarks, we can comment briefly on a version of revealed preference theory in which an individual's behaviour cannot be represented by a continuous utility function (see Debreu, 1954; Arrow, 1959; Richter, 1966; Sen, 1971; Herzberger, 1973). Does this version of revealed preference theory solve Samuelson's problem? Clearly, it meets a necessary condition for a satisfactory solution, namely the avoidance of the concept of utility. Nevertheless, it is unsatisfactory; it does not avoid the use of non-observational concepts or propositions. For example, in Arrow (1959) the domain of the 'weak axiom' is defined for all finite subsets. Clearly, it is not verifiable from observations of behaviour (see Sen, 1971 and 1973). The purpose of drawing attention to this version of revealed preference theory is to emphasize that Samuelson rejected ordinal utility theory because it is not observational. Therefore, a satisfactory solution to the Samuelson problem must not use any non-observational concepts or propositions.

16. The upshot of our analysis is that on consistency grounds Samuelson failed to solve his problems of deriving the three major results of ordinal utility theory without the use of non-observational concepts and propositions. The Samuelson Postulate and, by implication, the Samuelson Theory are not verifiable empirically from observations of market behaviour. The theory does not therefore satisfy the epistemological/methodological constraints which formed the major part of his rejection of ordinal utility theory.

17. If our criticism is valid, what options are open? First, the problem-situation can be amended by abandoning the methodological quest for empirical verification and clinging to an antecedent acceptance of ordinal utility theory. But, then, no valid argument can be advanced for the alleged methodological superiority of the Samuelson Theory over its predecessor. Moreover, the Samuelson problem of deriving the main results of ordinal utility theory without the use of non-observational concepts vanishes.

18. Second, the problem-situation can be altered by giving up the epistemological view that knowledge must be able to be proved or justified. With this option Samuelson's problem also disintegrates.

19. If, in fact, either option is taken, we must raise anew the question 'What is the problem to be solved by the Samuelson Theory?'

4.4 The Samuelson Theory as an explanation

1. A theory of consumer behaviour is concerned foremost with explanation. 'The basic purpose of the theory is to explain the demand vector $d(p,M)$ chosen by an individual when faced with a price vector p and an income M' (Arrow, 1959, p. 121). Therefore, its primary task is to answer the question 'Why did a consumer buy a particular bundle of goods?' A satisfactory answer must 'explain *why* he chose precisely *this* alternative rather than another one' (Kornai, 1971, p. 133).

2. Ordinal utility theory explains a consumer's behaviour in terms of his preferences and his given material circumstances – his income and given prices. It states that a consumer acted as he did because the bundle bought maximized his satisfaction in the given material circumstances. Putting it another way, all other bundles were not bought because they were either too expensive or would give less satisfaction. Thus, in explaining why a particular course of action was taken, why all other alternatives were not taken is also explained.

3. Is the Samuelson Theory an explanation, in this sense, of consumer behaviour? The answer should be 'Yes' if it is to be a replacement for ordinal utility theory. At this juncture, we cannot answer 'Yes' or 'No'. Because explanation was not identified by Samuelson as a major result of ordinal utility theory, he did not pose this question.[17] Therefore, we must attempt to construct an explanation of consumer behaviour in the spirit of the Samuelson Theory in order to answer this question.

4. In this section we shall argue that the Samuelson Theory is not an explanation in the sense that it explains why one bundle was bought and all other bundles were not. Moreover, we shall argue that two strategies which come readily to mind to repair this short-coming encounter serious difficulties. It should be noted that this criticism is on the logical plane; we are not considering here whether the Samuelson Theory is empirically true or not. Furthermore, because Samuelson did not identify explanation as a major result of ordinal utility theory and, therefore, as an aim of his problem-situation, our criticism is external and independent of the criticism set out in section 4.3 above.

5. Structurally an 'explanation' is a logical deduction.[18] The statement describing what is to be explained (called the *explicandum*) is the conclusion of an argument, while the statements which do the explaining (called the *explicans*) form the premises. In the explanation

of a particular act of consumer behaviour, the *explicans* consisting of an unrestricted universal statement is needed because we are interested not only in explaining a particular act but in all acts of consumer behaviour, by a single individual and by all individuals. Thus specific acts of consumer behaviour are explained as instances of a universal phenomenon. Initial conditions are required for two reasons. First, initial conditions in the form of singular statements describe the conditions which pertain to the particular act of consumer behaviour, for example the set of prices facing the individual. Second, since the *explicandum* is a singular statement, it is not deducible from a universal statement alone. For example, from 'If an object is a man, then it is mortal', we cannot derive 'John is mortal.' To do so, we need in addition the premise 'John is a man.' If the *explicandum* is derivable from the *explicans*, then the explanation is said to be logically complete.

6. Thus to give an explanation of consumer behaviour based on the Samuelson Theory, we need to use a universal statement, like, for example, the following:

> If a consumer is consistent in his buying behaviour up to time T, i.e. he has not violated the Samuelson Postulate, then at the price–income situation at time T, he buys the bundle which is consistent with his (past) behaviour, i.e. he does not violate the Samuelson Postulate. (To simplify the argument, we assume that the consumer spends his entire income in each buying situation.)

Given the *explicandum* 'John bought bundle X^t yesterday', we need the following initial conditions:

(1) John is a consumer;

(2) up to yesterday, John was consistent in his buying behaviour, i.e. in all the price–income situations that he has faced, there does not exist any pair of bundles $(X^a,\ X^b)$ of all the bundles bought such that $P^a X^a \geq P^a X^b$ and $P^b X^a \leq P^b X^b$ – in other words, the Samuelson Postulate has not been violated; and

(3) at time t, the consumer is facing the price–income situation (P^t, I^t).

7. Two important ideas are embodied in these premises. First, consistency of behaviour is defined as behaviour which does not 'violate' the Samuelson Postulate. This is in complete accordance with Samuelson's own interpretation of the postulate (see Samuelson,

1938a, p. 65). Second, we assume that behaviour is finite, i.e. a consumer at time T has bought only a finite number of bundles of goods.

8. From these premises we cannot derive the *explicandum* 'John bought bundle X^t yesterday.' The reason is that the explanation is logically incomplete.[19] It fails to explain why another bundle, from the set of bundles which, if bought, would not imply that John is inconsistent, was not bought. The incompleteness of this explanation is illustrated in the following example.

9. Consider the *explicandum* 'John bought bundle X^t yesterday.' In each time period with a given money income and given prices, John bought a particular bundle of goods. We can summarize this history of buying over three periods: at the price–income situation prevailing at time $t-1$, (P^{t-1}, I^{t-1}), he bought bundle X^{t-1}; at (P^{t-2}, I^{t-2}), he bought X^{t-2}; at (P^{t-3}, I^{t-3}), he bought X^{t-3}. This behaviour can be described as 'consistent' because for any pair of bundles from the above set there is no violation of the Samuelson Postulate. In addition, we assume that all income is spent in each buying situation. This history is depicted in Figure 4.2.

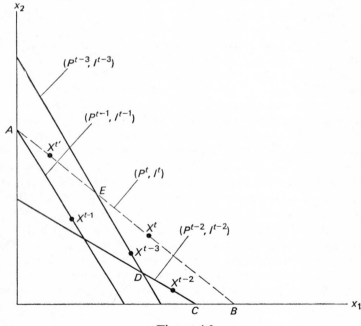

Figure 4.2

10. If the Samuelson Theory is to explain why X^t was bought at time t, it must explain why all other bundles were not bought. By assumption we are concerned only with those bundles which cost the same as bundle X^t at the price–income situation at time t. In other words, we must explain why all other bundles which cost the same as bundle X^t were not bought. If bundle $X^{t'}$ were bought, then the Samuelson Postulate is 'violated' and the consumer is said to be inconsistent since $P^{t-3}X^{t-3} > P^{t-3}X^{t'}$ and $P^tX^{t-3} < P^tX^{t'}$. (This is an elaborate way of saying that our explanation is false.) Similarly this inconsistency would appear if any bundle, represented by a point on the line segment AE, were bought. However, any bundle represented by a point on the line segment EB could be bought without 'violation' of the Samuelson Postulate. The explanation is therefore incomplete. We have not derived the *explicandum* 'John bought bundle X^t yesterday.' Behaviour has not been explained in terms of consistency of behaviour.

11. It should be pointed out that incompleteness is not problematic if the universal statement is interpreted as a rule of conduct. For example, if the consumer is told that he can buy whatever he desires provided he is consistent (in the sense defined by the Samuelson theory), then any bundle which does not cost more could be bought at the price–income situation prevailing at time T. This weakening of the completeness condition is unacceptable. The task for the Samuelson Theory is to explain consumer behaviour and not to prescribe the rules to which consumers must conform.[20]

12. In what circumstances, if any, is it possible to give a (complete) explanation of consumer behaviour using the Samuelson Theory? If we are willing to assume that the consumer has bought every bundle in some past price–income situation without being inconsistent in the above defined sense, then we can have a complete explanation. This assumption is at the heart of Little's attempt to explain consumer behaviour using the Samuelson Theory: 'If an individual's behaviour is consistent, then it must be possible to explain that behaviour without reference to anything other than behaviour' (1949, p. 97; see also 1950, ch. 2). The explanation is that the bundle X^t was bought yesterday at price–income situation (P^t, I^t) because in every past occurrence of that price–income situation, the bundle X^t was bought. To construct this explanation we are required to assume that the consumer has bought every possible combination of goods in the past, in other words an infinite number

of bundles of goods. This presumption is unacceptable if we recognize, as most of us do, that at any point in time a consumer has encountered a finite number of buying situations.

13. Another strategy is open to avert our criticism. It may be argued that completeness in explanation is desirable but not mandatory. Thus, in our example, we are content in being able to 'explain' that some bundle in the set representing a point on the line segment *EB* was bought. Although we wish to explain why X^t was bought, we are satisfied with narrowing the range of possibilities to those bundles represented by the point on the line segment *EB*. This strategy is purely *ad hoc* because we are changing the *explicandum* from 'John bought bundle X^t yesterday' to 'John bought some bundle represented by a point on the line segment *EB* yesterday' as the consequence of the inability to explain why X^t was bought.[21] Furthermore, the range of possibilities can only be specified after the explanation is constructed. In other words, the question is chosen to fit the answer.

14. It may be asked: Is the derivation of the single-valuedness of demand functions from the Samuelson Theory not equivalent, in our sense, to the explanation of consumer behaviour? The answer is 'No'. Recall that the single-valuedness of demand functions is derived from the Samuelson Postulate and demand functions which are given, in the sense that they are not explained. Thus the very thing that is to be explained is assumed as given. By contrast, in the Hicks–Allen version of ordinal utility theory, demand functions are explained in terms of the consumer's preferences and his material circumstances.

15. To summarize our criticism, the Samuelson Theory is not an explanation of consumer behaviour for the logical reason of incompleteness. However, if we are prepared to assume that a consumer can buy an infinite number of bundles, then the explanation is complete. It reduces to the simple statement that the consumer bought whatever he did because, when the price–income situation occurred in the past, he bought the same bundle and that his behaviour is consistent, in the sense of the Samuelson Postulate. In other words, the consumer is a creature of habit, and only of (consistent) habit. But is this not a high price for completeness?

16. In section 4.3 we argued that because the Samuelson Theory is not verifiable empirically, it is not a satisfactory solution to the problem of deriving the main results of ordinal utility theory without

the use of non-observational concepts. Independently of that criticism, the Samuelson Theory must be rejected as an alternative to, or replacement for, ordinal utility theory because the Samuelson Theory, unlike the ordinal utility theory, is not an explanation of consumer behaviour. Since Samuelson did not identify explanation as a major result of ordinal utility theory, and therefore did not include it as a part of his problem-situation, we must conclude that Samuelson misunderstood ordinal utility theory and has solved his problem only by mis-specifying the actual problem-situation facing him.

Chapter 5

A method of revealing preferences

5.1 The problem-situation of Samuelson (1948)

1. In 'Consumption Theory in Terms of Revealed Preference' (1948), Samuelson tackles the problem of constructing an individual's indifference map from observations of his market behaviour. The main object of the paper is to show that the problem is solved by revealed preference theory (Samuelson Theory) as presented in the original paper (1938a). In Samuelson's opinion, this exercise is a striking confirmation of his view that ordinal utility theory can be replaced by the new theory: 'The whole theory of consumer's behavior can thus be based upon operationally meaningful foundations in terms of revealed preference' (1948, p. 251).

2. Earlier, in the *Foundations of Economic Analysis* (1947, pp. 145–54), Samuelson addressed himself to a similar problem, of constructing an individual's indifference map from observations of his market behaviour. However, it was posed in the context of the theory of index numbers, in which ordinal utility theory and the existence of indifference maps are assumed. Therefore, it is a different problem from the 1948 problem-situation, which includes as a situational constraint the rejection of ordinal utility theory that was made in Samuelson (1938a). On this interpretation Little (1949), Houthakker (1950) and Georgescu-Roegen (1954a) are not fully justified in criticizing Samuelson for rejecting ordinal utility theory in his original paper (1938a) and accepting it for his later problem (1947) of constructing an indifference curve.

3. Our solution to the problem of understanding revealed preference theory as presented in Samuelson (1948) is to show that for Samuelson the theory is an adequate solution to the problem of

constructing an individual's indifference map from observations of his market behaviour. In section 5.2 we shall present Samuelson's solution to the problem. In section 5.3 we shall show that the solution is not satisfactory because it misuses the operationalist thesis upon which it depends, and, moreover, because this thesis is beset with insurmountable difficulties. As a major consequence of these criticisms we unravel the obscure relationship between the terms 'behaviour', 'preference', 'revealed preference' and 'as-if preference'. This chapter is independent of the criticisms of the Samuelson Theory that were set out in sections 4.3 and 4.4. However, we do rely on the rational reconstruction of the Samuelson Theory as given in sections 4.1 and 4.2.

4. First, we must consider whether both Samuelson (1938a) and Samuelson (1948) can belong to the same programme of research. It is highly questionable that the present aim of constructing an indifference map is a legitimate extension of a theory in which the use of utility or any other observational concept is diligently avoided. Recall that in the problem-situation of Samuelson (1938a), ordinal utility theory is rejected because it was considered non-observational. In its place Samuelson offered a new theory based on an observational postulate of consistency of behaviour. Since the present aim is seen as a proper application of the Samuelson Theory, the appraisal of ordinal utility in the problem-situation of Samuelson (1938a) must be a part of the new problem-situation (see section 2.2).

5. But if (ordinal) utility is not an observational concept, as Samuelson (1938a) argued, then by implication neither is indifference, since the concept of indifference is defined in terms of ordinal utility. What then is the point of constructing an indifference curve in the study of consumer behaviour? Has Samuelson changed his opinion about the acceptability of ordinal utility theory? If not, there is an inconsistency in the Samuelson Programme.

6. Putting it another way, consider what success there is in applying the Samuelson Theory to the construction of an indifference curve. If an indifference curve, which can be constructed from market observations, is observational, then the same should apply to ordinal utility theory. This implies that in proscribing the use of non-observational concepts, Samuelson had mistakenly swept aside ordinal utility theory to make way for his new theory. But if ordinal utility theory is not unsatisfactory, there is no longer a sufficient reason for devising the new theory.

7. That the construction of an indifference curve is an improper application of the new theory would be denied by Samuelson. This is apparent from his enthusiastic response to an earlier attempt by Little (1949), who, in the spirit of the Samuelson Theory, dispensed with non-observational concepts, and tried to construct what he called a 'behaviour line' from market observations in order to explain consumer behaviour solely in terms of behaviour. In fact, it was Little's efforts that stimulated Samuelson to offer (1948, p. 243) an alternative construction:

Recently, Mr. Ian M. D. Little of Oxford University has made an important contribution to this field. In addition to showing the changes in viewpoint that this theory may lead to, he has presented an ingenious proof that if enough judiciously selected price–quantity situations are available for two goods, we may define a locus which is the precise equivalent of the conventional indifference curve.

It is evident that the construction of a behaviour line (or indifference curve) is seen by Samuelson as an important and proper application of the new theory.

8. Because we disagree with Samuelson on the propriety of the present application of the Samuelson Theory to the construction of an indifference curve from market observations, it is necessary for us to document our position. The remainder of this section is devoted to this task. In addition, we offer a reinterpretation of the purpose and significance of the Samuelson Theory, one which reconciles, though not costlessly, the aforementioned conflict between the aim of constructing an indifference curve and the rejection of ordinal utility theory.

9. The opening paragraph of Samuelson (1948) reveals, without acknowledgment on the part of the author, a fundamental change in the interpretation of what was accomplished by his original paper of 1938 (1948, p. 243):

A decade ago I suggested that the economic theory of consumer's behavior can be largely built up on the notion of 'revealed preference'. By comparing the costs of different combinations of goods at different relative price situations, we can infer whether a given batch of goods is preferred to another batch; the individual guinea-pig, by his market behavior, reveals his preference pattern – if there is such a consistent pattern.

It is indeed surprising and none the less puzzling to find that prominence is given to the concept of preference. The Samuelson Theory, it seems, is about preferences after all. But reference to the preference concept was rejected in the formulation of the new theory. Preference, being a non-observational concept like utility, had no place in the study of consumer behaviour. Thus the Samuelson Postulate was presented as a postulate of consistency of behaviour and not of preferences. Assumptions about the existence and properties of preferences were carefully avoided. The interpretation that Samuelson gave to the postulate preserves the distinction that is made between behaviour and preferences: 'if an individual selects batch one over batch two, he does not at the same time select two over one' (1938a, p. 65). It is obvious that the postulate is not about preferences. If it were (substitute 'prefer' for 'select' in the above quotation), the postulate loses its novelty because the idea of consistency of preferences is central to ordinal utility theory. On this interpretation the Samuelson Theory cannot be a new theory, let alone be a solution to the problem of deriving the three major results of ordinal utility theory without the use of non-observational concepts.

10. In reply, it may be pointed out that the term 'preference' appeared in the addendum to the original paper of 1938. However, its use there was restricted. A special meaning was assigned to 'preference', presumably to dismiss any suggestion that its meaning is the same as that in ordinal utility theory. Thus the term 'prefer' (within quotation marks) was used as a synonym for 'select' in the original paper. The Samuelson Postulate now reads: 'the individual always behaves consistently in the sense that he should never "prefer" a first batch of goods to a second at the same time that he "prefers" the second to the first' (Samuelson, 1938b, p. 353). This use of the term 'preference' does not therefore contradict our contention that in its original conception the Samuelson Postulate is not about preferences.

11. Unfortunately, the special meaning of 'preference' is not maintained in the 1948 paper; the two separate meanings of the term are not distinguished. Confusion breaks out. Is the Samuelson Postulate about behaviour, about preferences, or both? What is the problem to be solved by revealed preference theory (the Samuelson Theory)?

12. In the 1948 interpretation of what was achieved in the first

paper (1938a), Samuelson states unequivocally that the theory is about preferences as well: 'By comparing the costs of different combinations of goods at different relative price situations, we can infer whether a given batch of goods is preferred to another' (1948, p. 243). This asserts that an inference of consistent preferences is drawn from observing consistent behaviour, i.e. behaviour which satisfies the Samuelson Postulate. This inference, which we shall examine in section 5.3, requires two essential assumptions. One is the ontological assumption that preferences exist. The other is that a consumer acts in accordance with his preferences subject to material circumstances. This is *almost* equivalent to assuming the truth of ordinal utility theory. All that is needed is to assume that preferences have the usual properties postulated in ordinal utility theory.

13. The major implication of Samuelson's present interpretation is that the Samuelson Theory cannot be a solution to the problem of deriving the three major results of ordinal utility theory without the use of non-observational concepts. The metaphysical assumption that preferences exist cannot be proved from observations of market behaviour, as is the case with the assumption that a consumer buys in accordance with his preferences subject to his material circumstances – that would be a circular argument. If it is acceptable for Samuelson to make these assumptions about unobservable entities, then it would be inconsistent of him to reject ordinal utility theory on the grounds that it posits the existence of unobservable entities.[1] Thus the constraint that non-observational concepts may not be used is dropped, at least implicitly. No significance can be attached to the derivation of the three major results from the Samuelson Theory, for if the interest were only in making the derivation, assuming them would suffice – every statement implies itself.

14. The 1948 paper marked the introduction of the term 'revealed preference' in the study of consumer behaviour; it did not appear in Samuelson (1938a), or in Samuelson (1938b). Henceforth, the theory presented in Samuelson (1938a) became known as 'revealed preference theory'. Rather than help to clear up the confusion over whether or not the Samuelson Theory is about preferences, the new term only adds to it. The term 'revealed preference' was coined in a sense in Samuelson (1947) in the discussion of the theory of index numbers but it was called *'revealed' preference*, therefore suggesting that it has something to do with preference in the sense of ordinal utility theory.

71

15. On a strict interpretation, the introduction of 'revealed preference' in the 1948 paper is terminological. The term 'reveal prefer' is equivalent to 'select' in Samuelson (1938a) and to 'prefer' (in the special sense) in Samuelson (1938b). Consequently there are now three equivalent definitions of the Samuelson Postulate:

(1) 'if an individual selects batch one over batch two, he does not at the same time select two over one' (Samuelson, 1938a, p. 65);

(2) 'he should never "prefer" a first batch of goods to a second at the same time that he "prefers" the second to the first' (Samuelson, 1938b, p. 353);

(3) if an individual reveal prefers a first batch to a second, he should not at the same time reveal prefer the second to the first (substituting 'reveal prefer' for 'select' in (1) with the appropriate grammatical changes).

On the interpretation of the Samuelson Postulate as one of behaviour, there is no informative value to be gained from asking whether or not X is revealed preferred to X' when one observes that when X was bought X' did not cost more and that when X' was bought X was too expensive. By definition, X is revealed preferred to X'.

16. It must be emphasized that revealed preference does not entail preference in the sense of ordinal utility theory. If it did, the concept of preference would be deprived of its explanatory power. Then Samuelson's remark on the hollowness of the Austrian version of utility theory would be appropriate: 'the consumer's market behavior is explained in terms of preferences, which are in turn defined only by behavior. The result can very easily be circular, and in many formulations undoubtedly is' (1947, p. 91). Consequently, an important question is ruled out: Is behaviour indicative of preference?

17. Unfortunately, Samuelson does not always observe this distinction between 'prefer' and 'revealed prefer'. For example, Samuelson speaks of a preference being revealed when revealed preference is intended (1948, p. 244; emphasis added – see also p. 249):

Through any observed equilibrium point, A, draw the budget-equation straight line with arithmetic slope given by the observed price ratio. Then all combinations of goods on or within the budget could have been bought in *preference to what was actually bought.*

This passage suggests that an observation of revealed preference implies preference.[2] Moreover, it is unclear what is meant by 'observed equilibrium point' unless we assume ordinal utility theory

18. To view the Samuelson Theory as the basis for the construction of an indifference curve or for the revelation of consistent preferences requires a fundamental change in the interpretation of the purpose of the theory. According to Samuelson (1938a), the theory is an observational theory which replaces the non-observational ordinal utility theory. But this is inconsistent with using the theory for the construction of an indifference curve, for two previously discarded assumptions must be reintroduced, that preferences exist and that a consumer's behaviour is governed by his preferences subject to his material circumstances. In effect, utility theory is back in favour; the Samuelson Theory did not replace it after all.

19. A reinterpretation of the purpose of the Samuelson Theory can now be given. It reconciles the aforementioned inconsistency.

20. The Samuelson Theory should be seen as a solution to the problem of how to justify ordinal utility theory using market observations. This problem is an offshoot of the Hicks–Allen Programme. It appears that Samuelson has taken the course of action which he dismissed earlier (1938a), that of reformulating ordinal utility theory in observational terms (see section 4.1). In this context the problem of constructing an indifference curve from market observations acquires significance. The assumptions that preferences exist and that a consumer's market behaviour is governed by his preferences and material circumstances, which are necessary if a positive solution is sought, are already made by ordinal utility theory. Thus the Samuelson Theory does not replace ordinal utility theory.

21. The upshot of our interpretation of the purpose of the theory is that the revolutionary significance of the Samuelson Theory is lost. The development of the theory does not represent a break with the tradition in economic theory in which consumer behaviour is explained in terms of preferences (and material circumstances). Consequently, the attendant philosophical and psychological controversies of utility theory, which Samuelson hoped to evade with his

observational theory, are not exorcised from the corpus of economic theory and, therefore, still await resolution or further elaboration.

22. In summary, the solution to our problem of understanding revealed preference theory as presented in Samuelson (1948) is the conjecture that the problem-situation of Samuelson (1948) is to construct an individual indifference map from market observations. An important situational constraint is the acceptance of ordinal utility theory, that a consumer's behaviour is governed by his preferences subject to his material circumstances. In this context the Samuelson Theory is interpreted as a means of revealing consistent preferences and not as a new theory; this change of interpretation was unwittingly given by Samuelson in the opening paragraph of the 1948 paper. Thus the present problem can be seen as a proper application of the Samuelson Theory.

23. In light of our analysis, let us set out the logic of the situation facing someone who disputes our claim that there is an inconsistency in the Samuelson Programme. First, he can argue that there is no inconsistency between the first paper (1938a) and the later one (1948). Second, he can reject the problem of constructing an individual's indifference map as a proper application of the Samuelson Theory and retain the 1938 interpretation of the Samuelson Theory as a new theory. Third, he can reject the 1938 interpretation and accept the 1948 interpretation that the Samuelson Theory is a solution to the problem of constructing an individual's indifference map from market observations. Fourth, he can reject both interpretations. By taking any one of the four options, a contribution to a better appreciation of the Samuelson Programme will be made.

5.2 Definition of indifference in terms of revealed preference

1. In this section we present, following Samuelson (1948), Samuelson's solution to the problem of constructing an individual's indifference map from observations of his market behaviour. It is sufficient for our purposes to describe his procedure for the construction of a single indifference curve.

2. We can observe in any buying situation the quantities of each good bought (x_1, x_2), the prices at which they were bought (p_1, p_2) and the total expenditure (I).

3. Let us assume that this set of observations is made for all

combinations of goods and that each combination is bought at one and only one set of relative prices (p_1/p_2). These sets of observations are summarized by the function:

$$p_1/p_2 = f(x_1, x_2), \tag{5.1}$$

which is assumed to be continuous with continuous partial derivatives.

4. For any combination (x_1, x_2) that is bought, the slope of the budget line at that point, $dx_2/dx_1 = -p_1/p_2$, substituted into equation (5.1), gives

$$dx_2/dx_1 = -f(x_1, x_2). \tag{5.2}$$

Equation (5.2) is a simple differential equation with continuous partial derivatives. Its solution is a system of curves. If we take the case where $p_1/p_2 = x_2/x_1$, the solution to equation (5.2) is a family of rectangular hyperbolae whose equation is $x_2\,x_1 = $ a constant (see Allen, 1938, ch. 16).

5. Samuelson's task is to show that the solution curves to equation (5.2) are indifference curves; between any two combinations on a single curve, the consumer is indifferent. The demonstration is accomplished by showing that an integral curve is the boundary between those combinations that are revealed preferred to a given combination A on the curve and those combinations to which A is revealed preferred.[3] Thus all combinations on the integral curve are not revealed preferred to A, and A is not revealed preferred to them; they are therefore indifferent to A.

6. Consider a combination A on an integral curve. We need to show that any other combination B on that curve is indifferent to A. This is accomplished with the use of two approximating methods.

7. The Cauchy–Lipschitz method approximates the integral-solution curve from below. We illustrate this method with reference to Figure 5.1.

8. At point A draw in the budget line at which that combination was bought; it cuts the vertical line running through B at B_1. B_1 is an approximation to B. By definition, A is revealed preferred to B_1 since A was bought and B_1 did not cost more at those prices and income at which A was bought. B_1 is certainly a crude approximation to the true value of the integral curve at the vertical line. A better approximation can be constructed.

9. On the line AB_1, take the point X^1 and draw in the budget line at which X^1 was bought. This line will cut the vertical line at B_2.

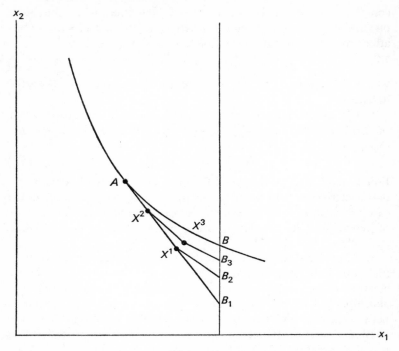

Figure 5.1

By definition of 'revealed preferred', A is revealed preferred to X^1, and X^1 is revealed preferred to B_2.

10. An even better approximation to B can be attained if we stop at point X_2 on the line AB_1, and draw in the corresponding budget line. Instead of extending this budget line to cut the vertical line, stop at say point X^3 draw in the corresponding budget line, and cut the vertical line at point B_3. Again, A is revealed preferred to X^2, X^2 is revealed preferred to X^3, and X^3 is revealed preferred to B_3. In general, if we take enough line segments we can approach the true solution at any desired degree of precision.

11. The conclusion that Samuelson draws from this approximation method is that A is revealed preferred to any approximate solution to B (1948, pp. 247–8, with notational changes):

> In economic terms, the individual is definitely going downhill
> along any Cauchy–Lipschitz curve. For just as A was revealed

to be better than B_1, so was it revealed to be better than X^1. Note too that B_1 is on the budget line of X^1 and is hence revealed to be inferior to X^1, which already has been revealed to be worse than A. It follows that B_2 is worse than A. By the same reasoning B_3 on the third approximation curve is shown to be inferior to A.

12. To show that B is indifferent to A, Samuelson proposes another approximation method. It is akin to the Cauchy–Lipschitz method except that it approximates the true solution from above. We illustrate this process with reference to Figure 5.2.

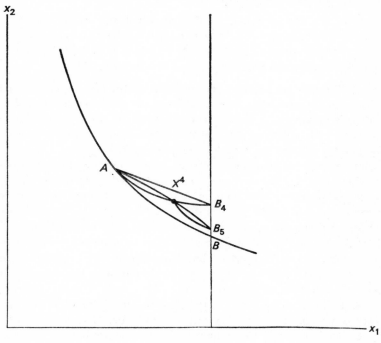

Figure 5.2

13. At point A rotate the budget line (of A) through all angles, tracing out an offer curve. Point B_4 is the point of intersection between the offer curve and the vertical line running through B. B_4 is the bundle bought at prices and income represented by the line segment AB_4. By definition, B_4 is revealed preferred to A.

14. A better approximation can be attained if we take point X_4, which is on the offer curve of A and which is bought at the prices and income represented by the line segment AX^4. At X^4 trace out an offer curve, letting it cut the vertical line at B_5.

15. In general, we can take as many intermediate points as we need to approximate the true solution at whatever degree of precision required.

16. The conclusion that is drawn from this approximation process is analogous to that of the Cauchy–Lipschitz process. Each approximate solution is revealed preferred to A (Samuelson, 1948, p. 251, with notational changes):

> Along the new process lines, the individual is revealing himself
> to be getting better off. For just as A is inferior to B_4, it is
> by the same reasoning inferior to X^4, which is likewise inferior
> to B_5; from which it follows that A is inferior to B_5.

17. We now put together the results from the two approximating processes to show that B is indifferent to A. From the Cauchy–Lipschitz process, A is revealed preferred to every approximate solution. In addition, by construction, each approximation is revealed preferred to any less precise approximation, i.e. every solution lying below it on the vertical line. From the other approximating process, each approximation is revealed preferred to A, but any less precise approximation is revealed preferred to a more precise approximation. As the consumer ascends the approximate solutions along the vertical line from below, he is getting better off, in the sense of 'revealed preferred', and as he descends the approximate solutions on the vertical line from above, he is getting worse off, in the sense that the preceding solution, though less accurate, is nevertheless revealed preferred to it.

18. Point B is the boundary between those bundles that are approximations to it from below, and therefore A is revealed preferred to them; and those bundles that are approximations to it from above are therefore revealed preferred to A. It is then assumed that between the set of bundles revealed preferred to A and the set of bundles to which A is revealed preferred, there exists a set of bundles, which are not revealed preferred to A and to which A is revealed preferred. This latter set is the indifference set of A. Hence B is not revealed preferred to A and A is not revealed preferred to B. In other words, B is indifferent to A. In general, any point on an

integral curve can be shown to be indifferent to any given point on that curve.

19. Georgescu-Roegen (1968, pp. 257–8) has remarked that Samuelson cautioned against identifying the curves constructed on the basis of revealed preference as indifference curves. This interpretation is incorrect in light of Samuelson's remarks that Little (1949) has devised a method for defining 'a locus which is the precise equivalent of the conventional indifference curve' (Samuelson, 1948, p. 243; see also p. 251).

20. The whole exercise in showing that an integral curve is an indifference curve demonstrates that the concept of indifference can be defined in terms of the observational concept of revealed preference. For Samuelson, the construction of an indifference curve is confirmation that 'The whole theory of consumer's behavior can thus be based upon operationally meaningful foundations in terms of revealed preference' (1948, p. 251).

5.3 Operationalism, indifference and revealed preference

1. The problem of deriving an indifference map from market observations is incompatible with the problem of devising a new theory which is free from non-observational concepts. If the Samuelson Theory is intended to solve the former problem, its purpose cannot be to replace ordinal utility theory because the problem of deriving an indifference map from observations of market behaviour arises in a theory which explains a consumer's behaviour in terms of his preferences and his material circumstances. Instead, the Samuelson Theory should be seen as an attempt to enhance the acceptability of ordinal utility theory, a theory which explains behaviour in terms of preferences and material circumstances. However, it remains to be seen whether the acceptability of ordinal utility theory can be enhanced in this way (see chapter 6).

2. Independently of these arguments, set out in section 5.1, as to whether or not Samuelson ever intended to replace ordinal utility theory, we shall here argue that Samuelson's solution to the problem of deriving an indifference map from observations of market-choice behaviour encounters a number of difficulties. At the root of these difficulties is a profound methodological confusion, which persists in the contemporary literature, over the relationships between the

terms 'behaviour', 'preference', 'revealed preference' and 'as-if preference'.

3. The construction of an indifference curve can properly be interpreted as an attempt to make operational the concept of indifference, i.e. to specify in terms of observable procedures the method by which one can determine whether or not a consumer is indifferent between two bundles of goods. This interpretation is in accordance with Samuelson's view (1948) that the term 'preference' was operationally defined in the original paper (1938a) as 'revealed preference'. Furthermore, the construction of an indifference curve is based logically on revealed preference. Thus, in concluding the 1948 attempt to define the concept of indifference in terms of revealed preference, Samuelson writes: 'The whole theory of consumer's behavior can thus be based upon operationally meaningful foundations in terms of revealed preference' (1948, p. 251).

4. Operationalism is a philosophical doctrine that establishes a criterion for determining which terms have or do not have empirical meaning and thus which terms can and cannot be a part of empirical science. It was first proposed by P. W. Bridgman (1927), a physicist, as a programme to ensure the stable, orderly growth of physics such that new discoveries would not necessitate a drastic revision of the fundamental concepts of physics.[4] Operationalism not only became influential in the physical sciences, but in the form of behaviourism, it attracted many social scientists who were eager to establish the scientific respectability of their respective disciplines.

5. The two major tenets of this doctrine as it applies to empirical science[5] are as follows:

(1) a term has empirical meaning if there exists a set of inter-subjectively observable and repeatable procedures or operations which determine the application of the term; and

(2) an empirically meaningful term is synonymous with the defining set of operations.

On the other hand, terms that are not defined operationally are deemed meaningless and, as a corollary, so are the statements and questions that contain those terms. It is therefore a matter of great importance, in the operationalist framework, to ascertain whether or not a question which is asked of empirical science is meaningful. A meaningful question is one which can be answered through the performance of the appropriate measuring operations (see Bridgman,

1927, pp. 28–31). Since an operational definition is designed to give meaning to a term, ambiguity in meaning must be avoided. Thus two sets of operations which apparently determine the application of a single term are in reality characterizing two different concepts.[6]

6. As we have already pointed out, Samuelson (1948) changed his interpretation of the purpose of the Samuelson Theory from being a new theory of consumer behaviour to a method of revealing consistent preferences. On the basis of this latter account, 'preference' is considered to be an operational term. Thus the statement 'A is preferred to B' is formulated in operational terms as follows: in the observed price–income situation at which A is bought, B is not bought but does not cost more. This operational statement can be abbreviated as 'A is revealed preferred to B.' To define operationally 'indifference' would further the goal of reformulating ordinal utility theory in observational terms.

7. Recall Samuelson's attempt to define the conventional indifference curve in terms of price–quantity data. Given some bundle A and some other bundle B, which both lie on a single integral curve, B is shown to be the common limit of two approximating processes. On one process line, every bundle is (revealed) preferred to bundle A and, on the other, bundle A is (revealed) preferred to every bundle on the line. In the limit, when the number of sub-intervals on each process line is infinite, the two process lines coincide with the consequence that bundle A cannot be shown to be (revealed) preferred to bundle B and bundle B cannot be shown to be (revealed) preferred to bundle A. In Samuelson's opinion this shows that bundle A is indifferent to bundle B and that, in general, indifference curves are the 'limiting loci of revealed preference' (1948, p. 245). Thus the concept of indifference is defined in terms of revealed preference.

8. Our objections to Samuelson's attempt to define operationally the concept of indifference are threefold. First, in carrying out the specified procedures for the construction of an indifference curve, Samuelson must assume that preferences do not change. This assumption is inconsistent with the other objectives of the problem-situation. Second, Samuelson misuses the operationalist thesis. The proposed set of operations which allegedly define 'indifference' cannot be performed. Third, logical difficulties, of which Samuelson is apparently unaware, confront operationalism as a programme designed to give empirical meaning to scientific terms. Because these

difficulties are inherent to operationalism, they invalidate all attempts to define operationally the terms 'indifference' and 'preference'.

9. To use the proposed set of operations to construct an indifference curve, Samuelson must assume that the individual's preferences do not change during the execution of these operations. This assumption is illegitimate in the problem-situation since the whole point of the exercise is to ascertain the individual's preferences from observations of his market behaviour. This is Joan Robinson's objection to the revealed preference approach (1962, p. 50, emphasis added):

> We can observe the reaction of an individual to two different sets of prices only at two different times. How can we tell what part of the difference in his purchases is due to the difference in prices and what part to the change in his preferences that has taken place meanwhile? There is certainly no presumption that his character has *not* changed, for soap and whisky are not the only goods whose use affects tastes. Practically everything develops either in inertia of habit or a desire for change.
>
> We have got one equation for two unknowns. *Unless we can get some independent evidence about preferences the experiment is no good. But it was the experiment that we were supposed to rely on to observe the preferences.*

Against this objection, Hahn commented, in a review of Kornai (1971), that, 'Unlike Professor Joan Robinson, Kornai understands that the empirical content of preference theory is that preferences are relatively stable' (1973, p. 326). This echoes Houthakker's remark that a violation of the axioms of revealed preference can be interpreted as a change of tastes: 'The axioms refer to a single individual at one instant of time, hence a violation of the axioms could always be ascribed to a change of tastes' (1961, p. 713). This misses the point of Robinson's complaint that the same set of procedures cannot be used both for the determination of preferences and for the determination of a change of preferences (see also Hicks, 1974, p. 10).

10. Furthermore, the assumption that preferences are not changing violates the situational constraint that non-observational concepts and propositions may not be used.

11. The second objection is that Samuelson's operational definition of 'indifference' is logically inadequate because the specified procedures for determining whether or not a consumer is indifferent

between two bundles cannot be carried out. In Samuelson's example, bundle *A* is shown to be indifferent to bundle *B* only when the two process lines coincide (see section 5.2). But because it is impossible to take an infinite number of sub-intervals on each process line, the two process lines never coincide in practice, and therefore an indifference relation between bundle *A* and bundle *B*, even if it exists for some independent reason, cannot be demonstrated with the proposed operations. Since the operations were proposed to give empirical meaning to the term 'indifference', one must conclude that from an operationalist point of view the statement 'bundle *A* is indifferent to bundle *B*' is meaningless, and cannot properly be used in scientific discourse.[7]

12. Against this criticism, it may be suggested that the term 'indifference' can be defined approximately. Thus an exact definition of 'indifference' may be seen to be the limit of successive approximations to it, each approximation being of a higher degree of precision.

13. In the example given in Samuelson (1948) for the number of sub-intervals (*n*) less than infinity, the two process lines do not coincide but touch at only one point (*A*). On the vertical line on which *B* is located, the two process lines cut at two different points; these two points are the boundaries of an interval in which *B* lies. An indifference bundle with respect to *A* is said to lie in this interval, which we shall call an 'indifference interval'. As the number of sub-intervals increase in number, the indifference interval gets smaller; that is to say, as the degree of precision increases, a better approximation to the indifferent bundle is defined in the sense that the boundaries of the indifference interval are moving in. Of course, it is not known whether or not bundle *B* is the indifferent bundle because it is only when *n* is infinity, that it is possible to show that bundle *B* is indifferent to bundle *A*.

14. To define operationally the term 'indifference' by approximations avoids the difficulty of the first proposal; the defining operations, or, more correctly, the defining sets of operations, can be executed in practice. Nevertheless, the second proposal fares no better. The idea of approximation suggests that with each degree of approximation a more precise definition of indifference is attained. However, each set of operations corresponding to a degree of approximation is actually determining a different concept of indifference because, from an operationalist point of view, a concept

is characterized fully and uniquely by its measuring operations: 'In general, we mean by any concept nothing more than a set of operations; the concept is synonymous with the corresponding set of operations' (Bridgman, 1927, p. 5). Consequently, operationalism cannot give a consistent account of corrections to measurements and improvements in methods of measurement (see Hempel, 1966, p. 94; and Gillies, 1972, p. 7).

15. In reply, it may be argued that our criticism against the use of approximations is nihilistic, ignoring the fact that all measurements are never precise but are always made at a certain degree of approximation. This point is not in dispute but it cannot be used to rebut our criticism.[8] Precision in defining terms is essential to the operationalist framework because operational definitions are designed to give empirical meaning to terms and, thereby, to determine the terms that can be properly used in empirical science and the questions that can be asked of empirical science.

16. The above proposed definition of 'indifference' by approximations should not be confused with the method of constructing, by successive approximations, an indifference map from observations of market behaviour that can be found in some well-known textbooks (Baumol, 1972; and Henderson and Quandt, 1971). It is asserted that using revealed preference theory a consumer's indifference map 'could be constructed with a high degree of accuracy (the "true" indifference map could be approximated as closely as is desired)' (Henderson and Quandt, 1971, p. 40). This exercise, which is in the spirit of Samuelson (1947, ch. 6), is not concerned with giving empirical meaning to the term 'indifference'. On the contrary, the meaningfulness of the term is not in doubt.

17. Similarly, the method proposed by Afriat (1967) and Diewert (1973) to construct an individual's utility function from observations of his market behaviour is not a satisfactory solution to the 1948 problem. Diewert uses the observed data to construct the coefficients of a linear-programming problem. If the objective function of the linear programme has a zero solution, then a utility function can be constructed on the basis of the solution. Unless the utility function is interpreted as an 'as-if' utility function, it must be assumed that an individual's utility function exists.

18. At this juncture, an operationalist is trapped in a predicament of his own making. He is faced with an unenviable choice situation: between a non-operational concept of indifference and a prolifer-

ation of concepts of indifference. The former is incompatible with the operationalist position, while the latter is of no theoretical value (see Hempel, 1966, p. 94). This dilemma, however, does not trouble those who have accepted both the concept of indifference and also ordinal utility theory as meaningful; they can quite consistently attempt to construct indifference curves (see, for example, MacCrimmon and Toda, 1969).

19. The third objection to Samuelson's attempt to define the concept of indifference in operational terms is more fundamental. The doctrine of operationalism is beset by logical difficulties. By their nature, these difficulties frustrate all attempts to define operationally theoretical terms. Samuelson's attempt to define operationally the term 'preference' is inextricably connected with his attempt to define operationally the term 'indifference'. The alleged successfulness of the former gave impetus to the latter, and furthermore the operational definition of 'indifference' is logically dependent upon the operational definition of 'preference'. Therefore, it is appropriate to discuss the logical difficulties of operationalism with respect to the operational definition of 'preference' as 'revealed preference'.

20. The basic criticism against operationalism is that all measurements (or measuring operations) presuppose theories; and theories, as is well known, are not verifiable from observations.[9] Consequently, theoretical terms are not made observational through operational definitions. We shall develop this line of criticism in our analysis of 'revealed preference' as an operational definition of 'preference'. Specifically, we shall argue that to use revealed preference as a measure of preference, a set of theoretical assumptions is required. We offer one set, a set which should come as no surprise since it is equivalent to ordinal utility theory. Hence, contrary to Samuelson's claims, 'preference' does not become an observational term through an operational definition of it.

21. The revelation of a consumer's preferences, or, more generally, the construction of a consumer's scale of preferences, should be considered in light of a long-standing interest in economics, one which dates back, before the advent of revealed preference theory, to the founding of utility theory. This is the interest in devising a method of determining whether or not a person's standard of living has improved, i.e. whether or not the person is better off with the consumption purchases of one period as compared with those of some other period(s).

22. Consider the statement:

John bought bundle X^0 at prices P^0 and spent his entire income
I^0 (A)

and the statement:

X^0 is revealed preferred by John to all bundles that did not cost
more at prices P^0 (B)

How are the two statements logically related? Two alternatives
come readily to mind. The first alternative is to regard (B) as definitionally equivalent to (A). This position follows from the
definition of 'revealed preference' that is given in the major contributions to the literature (see, for example, Arrow, 1959, p. 123;
Houthakker, 1950, p. 160; 1961, p. 707; Richter, 1966, p. 637;
1971, p. 32; Uzawa, 1960, p. 133):

A bundle X^0 is defined as *revealed preferred* to bundle X^1 if
bundle X^1 costs no more than bundle X^0 in the price–income
situation (P^0, I^0) in which X^0 is bought. (C)

A clarification of this definition is needed. Does the term 'revealed
preference' have anything to do with preference? Is it a shorthand
description of a certain type of market behaviour? If a distinction
between 'preference' and 'behaviour' is valued, then revealed preference as defined has nothing to do with preference; it is just
'revealed choice', and no more, to use Mishan's expression (1961,
p. 5, n. 1).

23. However, in the literature cited above there is a unanimous
'Yes' to both questions. The major consequence of this position,
which may or may not be intended, is the confusion of 'preference'
with 'behaviour': what is bought is preferred and what is preferred
is bought. A variant of this position considers the type of behaviour,
which is described, for example, by (A), to reveal the 'as-if' preference of the consumer (see, for example, McFadden, 1975, p. 402;
1976). Behaviour is then 'explained' in terms of the constructed
'as-if' preference ordering.[10] But, then, the 'as-if' preference ordering
must not be identified as the 'true' preference ordering and/or the
welfare ordering of the individual (see Sen, 1973, 1974).

24. If we wish to escape from the confusion of 'preference' with
'behaviour', we must turn to the second alternative, namely to view
(B) as a *conjecture* about the consumer's preference in light of the

behaviour which is described by (A). In contrast to the first alternative, whenever we affirm (A), we are not logically committed to affirm (B). We are therefore open to explore the conditions under which (B) is true, given (A). In other words, we are considering the question 'Is a consumer's market behaviour indicative of his preference?'

25. This question is clearly of no significance, and, moreover, is avoided by those who embrace the first alternative, which obscures the distinction between 'preference' and 'behaviour': behaviour, by definition, indicates preference. To do otherwise for an adherent of the first alternative is to be inconsistent. For example, Houthakker (1965, pp. 194–5) recognizes that market behaviour is not necessarily indicative of preference, i.e. not all choices are realized preferences. He attributes this possibility to the phenomenon of random choice. He then confines his analysis to choices that are preference-based, i.e. preferential choices. But in the context of revealed preference theory, using only observations of market behaviour, how can one distinguish preferential choice from random choice? Let us turn to the second alternative.

26. It was the concern with the truth of the conjecture that behaviour is indicative of preference which prompted Little to comment: 'The fact that an individual chooses *A* rather than *B* is far from being conclusive evidence that he likes *A* better' (1949, p. 92). For this reason, and because he thought a scientifically respectable theory about consumer behaviour should be stated in terms of behaviour, he tried to explain consumer behaviour solely in terms of behaviour. Although Little's attempt is unsuccessful, for reasons similar to those given in section 4.4 for the failure of Samuelson's theory to explain consumer behaviour, his remark that behaviour does not necessarily indicate preference underscores our main contention that the revelation of preferences from observations of market behaviour requires theoretical assumptions about the relationship between behaviour and preferences.[11] Behaviour is interpreted to signify preferences through the intermediary of theories.[12] Therefore, to treat the revelation of preference as dependent on an antecedent interpretation of behaviour is recognition that the interpretation may be wrong, and moreover that it may be corrected and improved upon.

27. It is our main contention that preference is revealed, so to speak, from observations of market behaviour only if certain

assumptions are made antecedent to the observation at hand.[13] These assumptions are theoretical, and are not therefore verifiable from observation. Thus a statement about preferences being revealed remains conjectural. Without these assumptions no valid inference can be made from observations. By observing behaviour, we cannot tell what are the objectives of the individual or the binding constraints of his choice situation.

28. Except by seeking refuge in the confusion of preference with behaviour, the operational definition of 'preference' as 'revealed preference' cannot be accomplished without the use of theoretical assumptions. This appropriation of theoretical assumptions is inconsistent with the operationalist demand for overt, observable operations. Thus Samuelson's objective of an observational theory of consumer behaviour is not served by the doctrine of operationalism.

29. We propose one set of assumptions which admits revealed preference as a measure of preference. This set entails the statement 'X^0 is revealed preferred by John to all other bundles that did not cost more at prices P^0' (B), given the observation described by the statement 'John bought X^0 at prices P^0 and spent his entire income I^0' (A). We must emphasize once again that this is only one set of assumptions and not the only set possible. We have chosen it because, as we shall see, it turns out to be equivalent to ordinal utility theory.

30. The theoretical assumptions can be divided into three categories:

(1) an assumption about the connection between a consumer's preferences and his market-choice behaviour;

(2) assumptions about the nature of the consumer's preferences; and

(3) assumptions about the nature of the price–income or choice situation that the consumer faced.

Although we shall refer frequently to the situation described by the statements (A) and (B), we shall formulate the theoretical assumptions in such a way that they are applicable to any attempt to measure preference by revealed preference.

31. Any proposed method of revealing or measuring preference from observations of market behaviour requires an assumption about the connection between a consumer's preferences and his market behaviour. This assumption serves two important functions.

First, it carries a commitment to the existence of preferences in one's ontology. Second, it postulates that a consumer's market behaviour is influenced by his preferences. Otherwise, we shall be constructing 'as-if' preferences.

32. Most writers on revealed preference theory assume that an inference can be made about his preferences from observations of an individual's market behaviour. Henderson and Quandt are representative of this opinion when they write: 'If his behavior conforms to simple axioms, *the existence and nature of his indifference map can be inferred from his actions*' (1971, p. 39; emphasis added). However, this cannot be done. In an observation of a market choice, we can record the quantities bought, the prices paid and the income spent. We cannot tell if that individual's behaviour is influenced by his preferences, and we cannot tell, for that matter, that his preferences do in fact exist. From observations of a consumer's market behaviour, no valid inference can be drawn about preferences, whether his or some other individual's. Therefore, if we wish to use observations of market behaviour to measure an individual's preferences, we must conjecture as follows:

(1) a consumer buys in the market what he prefers.

33. The behavioural assumption alone is insufficient to explain why the bundle bought by a consumer is preferred by him to all other bundles which did not cost more, under the assumption that the consumer *could have bought* any bundle within his means.

34. In addition, some assumptions about the nature of the consumer's preferences are needed:

(2) a consumer's preferences are defined over all bundles in any given price–income situation (completeness);

(3) if a consumer prefers one bundle to a second, he does not prefer the second to the first (asymmetry);

(4) a consumer prefers one bundle to a second if the first contains at least more of one good and no less of all other goods (non-satiation);

(5) given two goods, a consumer requires for each successive unit of one good that is given up an increasing amount of the second in order to maintain the same level of satisfaction while the quantities of all other goods do not change (strict convexity); and

    (6)   if a consumer prefers one bundle to a second and prefers the second to the third, he prefers the first to the third (transitivity).

35. Completeness of preferences means that, given any two bundles, a consumer either prefers one to the other or is indifferent between them; this assumption, which also goes under the names 'connectedness' or 'comparability', conveys what Georgescu-Roegen (1954b, p. 515) calls 'the belief in the reducibility of all wants' to a common basis. On the other hand, if preferences are not defined over X^0 and X^z and X^0 was bought and X^z did not cost more, it is false to assert that X^0 is (revealed) preferred by the consumer to X^z (see Sen, 1973, p. 8 (in LSE version)).

36. Although in any given price–income situation, asymmetry of preference is only required between X^0, the bought bundle, and any bundle that did not cost more, it becomes necessary to assume that a consumer's preferences are asymmetric for any pair of bundles if revealed preference is used as a general method to measure preference. It would be uninteresting, indeed, to assert that what a consumer bought is indicative of his preference if preferences were not asymmetric.

37. The condition of non-satiation explains why the consumer was observed to spend his entire income.

38. Strict convexity of preferences ensures that X^0, the bought bundle, is the preferred bundle in a free choice from the set of bundles that is determined by the given prices and income.

39. Although transitivity of preferences is not needed in any single attempt to measure preference with revealed preference, in the construction of a scale of preferences it denies the possibility of non-asymmetry from cropping up.

40. The behavioural assumption and the assumptions about the consumer's preferences entail that X^0, the bundle bought, is the preferred bundle in the given price–income situation under the additional assumption that the consumer had a free choice over all bundles defined by the prices and income. It would be false to say that X^0 is preferred to all bundles that did not cost more if in fact some of these bundles were not available to the consumer.

41. The assumption of free choice summarizes four separate assumptions about the choice situation that is faced by a consumer:

    (7)   each good is perfectly divisible;

(8)   it is possible for a consumer to buy any combination of goods that he can afford;

(9)   the prices of goods cannot be influenced by the consumer; and

(10) the price per unit of each good is the same regardless of the quantities purchased.

42. If goods are not perfectly divisible, or if the market will not sell to the consumer any bundle that he can afford, the conjecture that the bought bundle is the preferred bundle in the given price–income situation is false.

43. If prices of goods are open to the influence of the consumer, the bought bundle may not be the preferred bundle but will instead be one of the preferred set of bundles in the given price–income situation.

44. If quantity discounts are available to the consumer, the bundle that is bought, say X^z, may not be the preferred bundle in the given price–income situation because, though the preferred bundle X^0 belonged to the set defined by the price–income situation at which X^z was bought, if the consumer had tried to buy X^0, the prices at which he could buy it would mean that he is spending beyond his means.

45. Under what conditions is it true that X^0 is preferred to all bundles that did not cost more, given the observation that X^0 was bought and the consumer spent his entire income? The statement that 'X^0 is preferred to all bundles that did not cost more' is true if the above ten assumptions (plus the appropriate initial conditions) are true. Since these assumptions are not verifiable by observation, it cannot be demonstrated that X^0 is the preferred bundle in the given price–income situation, even if it is true.

46. Three reasons explain why the assumptions are not open to verification by observation. First, the assumptions are said to apply to every instance of market choice of all individuals, not only that of a single individual. Second, the behavioural assumptions and the assumptions about the nature of preferences contain the non-observational concept of preference. Moreover, assumptions (7), (9) and (10) above are not verifiable because it is impossible to consider every possible combination of goods. Third, assumption (8) cannot be verified because whether or not the market is willing to sell any amount of goods to an individual is dependent on the 'good will'

of all participants in the market transaction. It cannot be demonstrated that a consumer could buy a particular combination of goods before he does so.

47. This latter point focuses on an assumption which goes unmentioned in the literature. It is the presupposition that in any market transaction every agent expects to 'play by the rules' and expects others to do so as well. An atmosphere of trust hovers over a market transaction.

48. Let us now draw together the various strands of our argument against the operational definition of 'preference' and set out the logic of the situation that faces someone who may wish to choose between the two interpretations of 'revealed preference': as a definition of a certain type of market behaviour and as a conjecture about a consumer's preferences in light of observations of the consumer's market behaviour. On the first account, revealed preference theory is about behaviour and has nothing to do with preference. On this interpretation, 'the use of the word "preference" in revealed preference would represent an elaborate pun' (Sen, 1973, pp. 2–3 (in LSE version)). On the second account, revealed preference is admitted as a measure of preference, a measure which may be incorrect and which may be improved upon. Since for logical reasons it rests on a preference-based theory of consumer behaviour, and because the theory cannot be verified before the measure is used, 'revealed preference' is not an operational definition of 'preference'.

49. It is difficult to discern from Samuelson's writings whether 'revealed preference' is about behaviour or about preference. Contradictory evidence abounds. On the one hand, a passage such as 'if an individual selects batch one over batch two, he does not at the same time select two over one' (Samuelson, 1938a, p. 65; see also 1938b, p. 353) suggests that revealed preference is not about preferences. On the other hand, there are passages which support the opposing view, for example: 'Through any observed equilibrium point, A, draw the budget-equation ... Then all combinations of goods on or within the budget line could have been bought in preference to what was actually bought' (Samuelson, 1948, p. 244). Again, consider the following description of an approximating process line, which is used in Samuelson's construction of an indifference curve: '[it] definitely reveals the economic preference of the individual at every point' (Samuelson, 1948, p. 249). Instead of

delving further into what Samuelson 'really' meant by revealed preference, we shall draw out the consequences of each interpretation for the Samuelson Programme.

50. If Samuelson considers revealed preference to be just a definition of a certain type of market behaviour, what he attempted to construct is not an indifference curve. Moreover, it raises the question 'What is Samuelson's objective in constructing an indifference curve based on revealed preference, which has nothing to do with preference?'

51. If Samuelson did not realize that measurements presuppose theories, then the inconsistency of operationalism implies that Samuelson has failed to define operationally the terms 'preference' and 'indifference'. He has therefore not made any progress towards the realization of his goal of creating an observational theory of consumer behaviour.

52. If Samuelson did recognize that revealed preference as a measure of preference requires the acceptance of a preference-based theory of consumer behaviour, antecedent to its application, fresh doubts are raised about the purpose and significance of 'revealed preference' and of the Samuelson Theory. For example, how does 'revealed preference' serve Samuelson's objective of an observational theory of consumer behaviour, in light of our criticism of operationalism? Second, consider, once again, the statement 'X^0 is *revealed preferred* by John to all bundles that did not cost more at prices P^0.' Given ordinal utility theory, this statement is equivalent to the statement 'X^0 is *preferred* by John to all bundles that did not cost more at prices P^0.' This latter statement is in fact the explanation given by ordinal utility theory of *why* it was observed that John bought X^0. Therefore, to say that preference is revealed by behaviour is to stand ordinal utility theory on its head! Consequently, Samuelson is incorrect and misleading to assert that 'The whole theory of consumer's behavior can thus be based upon operationally meaningful foundations in terms of revealed preference' (1948, p. 251). The term 'revealed preference' acquired significance (or 'meaning', if you wish) in the context of a preference-based theory of consumer behaviour such as ordinal utility theory.

53. In light of the preceding analysis, we shall now examine Samuelson's interpretation that the Samuelson Theory is a method of revealing consistent preferences (1948, p. 243):

A method of revealing preferences

By comparing the costs of different combinations of goods at different relative price situations, we can infer whether a given batch of goods is preferred to another batch; the individual guinea-pig, by his market behavior, reveals his preference pattern – if there is such a consistent pattern.

In other words, behaviour which conforms to the Samuelson Postulate implies that the consumer's preferences are consistent, and, on the other hand, behaviour which violates the Samuelson Postulate implies that the consumer's preferences are inconsistent.

54. Following the preceding argument, that if revealed preference is a measure and not an operational definition of preference, theoretical assumptions are required, we shall here argue that behaviour which violates the Samuelson Postulate does not imply that the consumer's preferences are inconsistent; second, that behaviour which satisfies the postulate does not imply that the consumer's preferences are consistent; and third, that inconsistent preferences may not necessarily be detected through the use of the Samuelson Postulate. We shall conclude that the Samuelson Postulate should be seen as one of a number of possible ways to test ordinal utility theory.

55. Consider, first, what is implied by a falsification of the Samuelson Postulate: $P^1X^1 > P^1X^2$ and $P^2X^1 \leq P^2X^2$, where X^1 was bought at price–income situation (P^1, I^1), X^2 was bought at price–income situation (P^2, I^2) and the consumer's income was spent in each situation. This state of affairs is usually interpreted to mean that inconsistent preferences are revealed. However, in the light of our analysis of revealed preference as a measure of preference, this inference is wrong. Given ordinal utility theory, which is equivalent to the ten assumptions given above, the falsification implies that at least one statement in the set formed by the conjunction of these ten assumptions and the appropriate initial conditions is false. And since the set of assumptions is not verifiable, there is wide latitude in deciding which assumption(s) is (are) false.[14] Thus only if all assumptions other than asymmetry of preferences are true, does the falsification of the Samuelson Postulate imply that the consumer's preferences are inconsistent, i.e. non-asymmetric. With a bit of ingenuity and good luck, we may be able to devise ways to criticize independently some of these assumptions.

56. Houthakker, in more charitable vein, has suggested that

a violation of the axioms of revealed preference can be interpreted as a change of taste: 'The axioms refer to a single individual at one instant of time, hence a violation of the axioms could always be ascribed to a change of tastes' (1961, p. 713). We have already disputed the validity of the argument; while this interpretation avoids passing judgment on the rationality of the consumer, it avoids the uncomfortable conclusion that violation implies that some part of the ordinal utility theory of consumer behaviour is false. It is unfortunate that the truth or falsity of the Samuelson Postulate is bound up with discerning whether or not a consumer has consistent preferences. What is, in fact, under consideration in testing the Samuelson Postulate is the truthfulness of the ordinal utility theory which is used to interpret (explain) consumer behaviour.

57. Similarly, behaviour which satisfies the Samuelson Postulate does not mean that the consumer's preferences are consistent or that ordinal utility theory is true. We cannot anticipate the result of the next attempt to test the Samuelson Postulate or of other tests of ordinal utility theory. We can, if we so choose, conjecture that ordinal utility is a true explanation of consumer behaviour and, by implication, that consumer preferences are consistent provided we acknowledge that behavioural evidence yields no proof.

58. To further strengthen our argument that falsification of the Samuelson Postulate does not mean the consumer's preferences are inconsistent, we offer examples of a consumer's market behaviour which violates the Samuelson Postulate, but the consumer, nevertheless, does have consistent preferences. These examples should dispel any lingering doubts that revealed preference as a measure of preference acquires significance only in the context of a preference-based theory of consumer behaviour.

59. By recognizing that some part of ordinal utility theory other than the assumption of consistent preferences is false, we can conceive of situations where a consumer does not buy the optimal bundle in price–income situations as ordinal utility theory expects.[15] We illustrate with four basic cases in Figure 5.3.

60. In case 1b, the consumer bought the optimal bundle, in the sense of ordinal utility theory, in price–income situation (P^0, I^0) but did not do so in (P^1, I^1). In case 2a, the situation is reversed: the optimal bundle which corresponds to (P^1, I^1) is bought but not in the case of (P^0, I^0). In case 2b, we have three sub-cases in which the

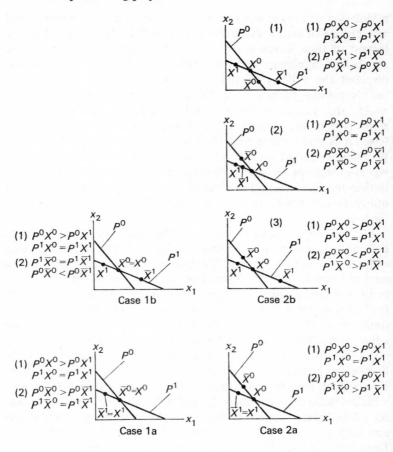

X^i = bundle bought in situation (P^i, I^i) $i = 0,1$
$\bar{X}^i$ = optimal bundle in situation (P^i, I^i) $i = 0,1$
All income is spent in each situation

Figure 5.3

optimal bundle is not bought in both situations. In case 1a, the optimal bundle is bought in each price–income situation.

61. In case 1b, the consumer's market behaviour violates the Samuelson Postulate: $P^0X^0 > P^0X^1$ and $P^1X^0 = P^1X^1$. Inconsistent preferences are allegedly revealed. However, if the consumer did buy the optimal bundle in each situation, his market behaviour would not

have violated the Samuelson Postulate; this does not mean, of course, that ordinal utility theory is a true explanation of consumer behaviour. Case 2a is the reverse of case 1b.

62. In case 2b, the optimal bundle is not bought in either situation. In sub-cases (1) and (2), actual behaviour violates the Samuelson Postulate but optimal behaviour would not. In sub-case (3), actual behaviour violates the Samuelson Postulate but optimal behaviour would not because the two situations are incomparable with respect to the Samuelson Postulate.

63. In case 1a, where actual behaviour is optimal (with respect to ordinal utility theory), then violation of the Samuelson Postulate does imply that the consumer's preferences are inconsistent. But, since we cannot prove that all parts of ordinal theory is true except for the assumption of consistent preferences, violation of the Samuelson Postulate implies only that ordinal utility theory is false. There are grave difficulties in detecting which part of a theory is false and, moreover, in deciding how to repair that defect when it is discovered.

64. In addition, there are practical difficulties in using the Samuelson Postulate to detect the existence of inconsistent preferences or to test the truth of ordinal utility theory. If, for example, incomes are increasing, the scope and applicability of the Samuelson Postulate is severely restricted. In order to refute the Samuelson Postulate, we have to observe that the two bundles under consideration are available in both price–income situations. And since this is unlikely in the presence of growing incomes, there will be few cases of falsification of the Samuelson Postulate.[16] Furthermore, the quality and quantity of observations of market-choice behaviour severely restrict the opportunities of testing ordinal utility theory with the Samuelson Postulate.

65. Our present discussion of the usefulness of the Samuelson Postulate as a test of consistency of preferences has, in effect, led us to the position that the Samuelson Postulate should be seen as a test of ordinal utility theory, underscoring our major contention that measurements presuppose theories. On this view we are no longer restricted to testing ordinal utility theory only in market situations. Two important consequences follow. First, the domain of the Samuelson Postulate as a test should be extended from being applicable only to budget situations to all finite subsets. This gives an added dimension to Sen's argument (1971, pp. 310–12) that this

extension renders redundant the so-called 'strong axiom of revealed preference', the strong form of the Samuelson Postulate, and greatly simplifies the number of so-called 'rationality conditions'. By enlarging the domain of applicability of the Samuelson Postulate, the scope for testing ordinal utility theory, for those who wish to do so, is increased. For example, the Samuelson Postulate can be applied to experimental choice situations. Second, it should be recognized that there are other tests of ordinal utility theory. On our view that revealed preference as a measure of preference presupposes theoretical assumptions, tests can be devised to evaluate assumptions other than that of consistency of preferences. For example, we can question a consumer about his preferences, test whether each good is perfectly divisible, test whether a consumer can buy what he chooses if he can afford it, and so on.

66. In summary, Samuelson's problem of constructing an individual's indifference map from observations of his market behaviour (1948) is seen as an attempt to make operational the concept of indifference. His solution is to define indifference in terms of revealed preference. The latter concept is considered as the operational form of the concept of preference. The solution is therefore an application of the doctrine of operationalism which establishes a criterion for determining which concepts have empirical meaning in terms of observable and repeatable procedures.

67. We have argued that the solution is unsatisfactory because it violates the situational constraint that non-observational concepts and propositions may not be used. First, in the construction of an indifference curve, it must be assumed that preferences are not changing. This is invalid because the point of the exercise is to determine the individual's preferences. Moreover, this assumption cannot be proved from observations. Second, the proposed set of operations for the construction of an indifference curve cannot be carried out in practice. To assume that an indifference curve can be constructed through the application of these operations an infinite number of times violates the situational constraint against the use of non-observational propositions. According to operationalism, indifference is not meaningful empirically. Third, to construct an indifference curve by approximations leads to a proliferation of indifference concepts which are of no theoretical value. Fourth, the doctrine of operationalism is beset by a serious logical difficulty. All operational definitions require the use of theoretical (non-observ-

ational) assumptions which are not verifiable from observations. Except by confusing 'preference' and 'behaviour', the operational definition of 'preference' as 'revealed preference' violates the situational constraint against using non-observational propositions. Therefore, the Samuelson Programme is not well served by the doctrine of operationalism.

Chapter 6

The observational equivalent
of ordinal utility theory

6.1 The problem-situation of Samuelson (1950b)

1. In 'The Problem of Integrability in Utility Theory' (1950b) Samuelson gives a third interpretation of the revealed preference approach, one which is maintained in his subsequent work (1953) and in his methodological writings (1963, 1964, 1965a). We shall refer to this interpretation as 'the 1950 interpretation', or 'the 1950 problem-situation'.

2. According to the 1950 interpretation, the problem of the revealed preference approach is to derive the full empirical implications of ordinal utility theory. The Samuelson Theory is seen (by Samuelson) as a tentative, though unsatisfactory, solution to this problem. As we have pointed out in section 4.1, this is the interpretation usually given in the literature. Houthakker (1950), which draws upon the revisions and extensions in Samuelson (1947, 1948) and Little (1949), is said to solve the problem.

3. The Samuelson Theory is an unsatisfactory solution to the 1950 problem-situation because it is a necessary rather than a sufficient condition for ordinal utility theory (see Samuelson, 1950b, p. 370). By reformulating the postulate of consistency of behaviour, Houthakker proves that revealed preference theory, as revised, is logically equivalent to ordinal utility theory. Thus Samuelson concludes that Houthakker has found the necessary and sufficient observational conditions for ordinal utility theory, completing the programme which he, Samuelson, initiated 'a dozen years ago [aimed at] arriving at *the full empirical implications for demand behaviour of the most general ordinal utility analysis*' (Samuelson, 1950b, p. 369).

100

4. Notwithstanding Samuelson's opinion to the contrary, there is the problem of interpreting the Samuelson Programme. In the 1950 interpretation, the Samuelson Theory is considered as a tentative but unsatisfactory solution to the problem of deriving the full empirical implications of ordinal utility theory. By contrast the original 1938 paper interprets the new theory as an adequate solution to the problem of deriving the main results of ordinal utility theory without the use of utility or any other non-observational concept. The 1950 interpretation cannot be viewed as an attempt to clarify the earlier interpretation. In the 1938 paper ordinal utility theory is rejected and a replacement is sought. On the other hand, ordinal utility theory is an unobjectionable part of the 1950 problem-situation. It is self-defeating to search for the full empirical implications of ordinal utility theory and to dispense with the last vestiges of the utility concept. A positive solution to the 1950 problem-situation implies that in the same programme the problem-situation of the 1938 paper is unsolvable. Thus the programme of research is inconsistent.

5. There is some strong documentary evidence that supports our point of view. The problem of integrability, which is often interpreted to be the concern with the recovery of an individual's utility function from his market-demand functions, is dismissed by Samuelson as an illegitimate and irrelevant concern in the context of the new theoretical framework (1938a, p. 68):

> Concerning the question of integrability, I have little to say.
> I cannot see that it is really an important problem, particularly
> if we are willing to dispense with the utility concept and its
> vestigial remnants . . . I should strongly deny, however, that for
> a rational and consistent individual integrability is implied,
> except possibly as a matter of circular definition.

It is clear that this position is abandoned by Samuelson in his 1950 interpretation. Here he states unequivocally that the question of integrability was a legitimate concern in the context of his new approach and, moreover, that it was not dealt with satisfactorily in the earlier paper (1950b, p. 370):

> I soon realized that this [the 'weak axiom'] could carry us
> almost all the way along the path of providing new foundations
> for utility theory. But not quite all the way. The problem of

integrability, it soon became obvious, could not yield to this weak axiom alone.

6. The inconsistency in Samuelson's various interpretations was already apparent to Houthakker (1950, p. 159) from his reading of Samuelson (1938a) and Samuelson (1947):

> Though originally intended 'to develop the theory of consumer's behaviour freed from any vestigial traces of the utility concept,' i.e., as a substitute for the 'utility function' and related formulations, it has since tended to become complementary to the latter; in his *Foundations* Professor Samuelson uses it to express the empirical meaning of utility analysis, to which he apparently no longer objects.

He did not, however, find the inconsistency sufficiently serious to raise such questions as: What is the problem to which revealed preference theory (the Samuelson Theory) is a solution if Samuelson no longer wishes to purge all traces of utility from the theory of consumer behaviour? Why does Samuelson no longer object to ordinal utility theory?

7. Nevertheless, the inconsistency which results from the change in Samuelson's interpretation of the revealed preference approach cannot be ignored because it casts considerable doubt on the prevailing view that the creation of revealed preference is a landmark development in the history of the theory of consumer behaviour (see, for example, Schumpeter, 1954; Houthakker, 1961; and Arrow, 1967). It is said that through this development the theory of consumer behaviour became paradigmatic in economics because it succeeded in severing its logical and connotative ties with philosophy and psychology, disciplines which hitherto had been sources of great controversies not only in the theory of consumer behaviour but also in other areas of economics (see, for example, Houthakker, 1961; and Samuelson, 1963, 1964, 1965a).

8. This inconsistency of the Samuelson Programme can be resolved in one of three ways. First, it can be argued that there is no inconsistency in the various interpretations by pointing out the sources of the misinterpretation of his views. Second, the 1938 interpretation can be retained by arguing that the programme is designed to free the theory of consumer behaviour from the concept of utility, and therefore one can reject the Houthakker formulation as an unaccept-

able development within the context of the new framework. Moreover, it must then be explained why, on further consideration, the Houthakker result and the 1950 interpretation are rejected. Third, the Houthakker reformulation and the 1950 interpretation can be accepted. However, it must be explained why the 1938 interpretation is rejected. Fourth, the 1938 interpretation and the 1950 interpretation can be rejected. Thus, by solving this problem of interpretation, a significant contribution to a much needed re-assessment of the importance of the revealed preference approach to the theory of consumer behaviour will be made.

9. Independently of the above argument, i.e. that there is an inconsistency in Samuelson's various interpretations of his programme, we shall now examine the 1950 interpretation of revealed preference theory as a solution to the problem of discovering the full empirical implications of ordinal utility theory.

10. The aim of the revealed preference approach, according to Samuelson (1950b), is to derive empirical implications from ordinal utility theory. It should be noted that this is not a new direction in Samuelson's work. It is the aim of his article 'The Empirical Implications of Utility Analysis' (1938c) which was published in the same year in which he first proposed his new approach.

11. But Samuelson did point out that the interest in ordinal utility theory does not and should not prejudice his case for a new foundation for the theory of consumer behaviour which is free from any traces of the utility concept (1938c, p. 346):

> Recently I proposed a new postulational base upon which to construct a theory of consumer's behavior. It was there shown that from this starting point could be erected a theory which included all the elements of the previous analysis. There I expressed my opinion as to the advantages from a methodological point of view of such a reorientation. Completely without prejudice to such considerations I should like here to indicate the mathematical simplicities which suggested themselves from that investigation. That is to say, even within the framework of the ordinary utility- and indifference-curve assumptions it is believed to be possible to derive already known theorems quickly, and also to suggest new sets of conditions.

Thus the 1950 interpretation is the first time that Samuelson regards the derivation of empirical implications of ordinal utility theory as part of his new approach.

12. It is not immediately obvious how the derivation of empirical implications of ordinal utility theory fits into a programme which is directed to the creation of a theory of consumer behaviour that is free from any reliance on the concept of utility. Or, more pointedly, how is revealed preference theory logically related to ordinal utility theory? The answer comes from an appreciation of the difference in Samuelson's thinking between the expressions 'full empirical implications' and 'empirical implications'.

13. The importance of deriving the full empirical implications of ordinal utility theory is a consequence of Samuelson's methodology. Accordingly, we shall present a detailed account of this situational constraint. Although our presentation of Samuelson's methodology is drawn mainly from his post-1950 writings on methodological issues, it is not in violation of our procedure of reconstructing the problem-situation as the theorist saw it. We remarked earlier that Samuelson frequently uses his 1950 interpretation of revealed preference theory to clarify and defend his methodological position.

14. According to *descriptivism*, of which Samuelson's methodology is a variant,[1] a theory is just a description of observable experience, a convenient and mnemonic representation of empirical reality (see Samuelson, 1952, p. 57; 1963, p. 236; 1965a, p. 1171). Knowledge consists essentially of observational reports: 'Every science is based squarely on induction – on observation of empirical fact' (Samuelson, 1952, p. 57). The search for the foundations of knowledge solves the twin problems 'What is knowledge?' and 'How do we attain (true) knowledge?' For Samuelson (1965a, p. 1168), knowledge is what can be proved from observations.

15. Samuelson defines a theory (called '*B*') 'as a set of axioms, postulates, or hypotheses that stipulate something about observable reality' (1963, p. 233), and which can be either refuted or confirmed in principle by observation.[2] It has a set of consequences (called '*C*') which is logically implied by the theory and a set of assumptions (called '*A*') which logically implies the theory.

16. 'If *C* is the complete set of consequences of *B*, it is identical with *B*' (Samuelson, 1963, p. 234), and if *A* is the minimal set of assumptions that give rise to *B*, then *A* is identical to *B*. According to Samuelson, if *C* and *A* are given the above interpretation, they are logically equivalent to *B*, and by transitivity of equivalence, to

each other. Therefore, the degree of 'realism', 'factual correctness', 'empirical validity', or 'truth', of any one of A, B or C is shared by the other two and it is a contradiction to maintain that any one of A, B or C can have a degree of realism which is different from the others.

17. In case only some part of A, B or C has empirical validity, Samuelson gives the following argument.

18. Consider a proper sub-set (called '$C-$') of the consequence set C and let set A be a proper sub-set of the enlarged assumption set (called '$A+$'). Symbolically, he represents this relationship as follows:[3]

$$A+ \supset A \equiv B \equiv C \supset C-. \qquad (6.1)$$

If C has 'complete (or satisfactory) empirical validity' (Samuelson, 1963, p. 234), then so does the theory B and the assumption set A. However, we cannot say anything about $A+$ 'unless its full content, which we may call $A+ \equiv B+ \equiv C+$, also have empirical validity. If that part of $C+$ which is not in C is unrealistic in the sense of being empirically false at the required level of approximation, then $A+$ is definitely the worse for it' (Samuelson, 1963, p. 234). Accordingly, it is absurd to maintain that if only some parts of C are valid, then B and A are important though invalid. The only thing to do, Samuelson says, is to eliminate that part of B and A corresponding to the invalid part of C and retain:

$$A- \equiv B- \equiv C-. \qquad (6.2)$$

19. Since the object of a theory is to represent observable experiences, a scientifically respectable theory, according to Samuelson, must be expressed in observational language, i.e. a theory should be logically equivalent to its empirical consequences C, which are statements of facts. On the other hand, a theory is inferior if it is not expressed in observational language.

20. This viewpoint, concerning the growth and development of empirical science, can be elaborated upon with the aid of Figure 6.1, which is adapted from Samuelson (1963). Each entry is a proper subset (or consequent, since the notation is used ambiguously by Samuelson) of the entry above it. In the northerly direction, there is increasing generality or universality. At each level an attempt is made to establish a logical equivalence between a theory and its assumptions and consequences, i.e. there is a search for the necessary and sufficient conditions for the theory. Specifically, the Cs are said

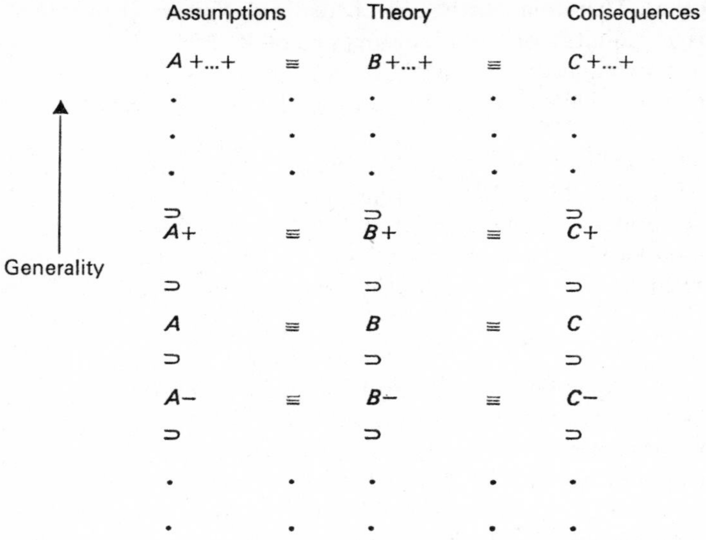

	Assumptions		Theory		Consequences
	$A+...+$	$\equiv$	$B+...+$	$\equiv$	$C+...+$
	.	.	.	.	.
	.	.	.	.	.
	.	.	.	.	.
	$\supset$		$\supset$		$\supset$
	$A+$	$\equiv$	$B+$	$\equiv$	$C+$
	$\supset$		$\supset$		$\supset$
	A	$\equiv$	B	$\equiv$	C
	$\supset$		$\supset$		$\supset$
	$A-$	$\equiv$	$B-$	$\equiv$	$C-$
	$\supset$		$\supset$		$\supset$
	.		.	.	.
	.		.	.	.

Generality (↑)

Figure 6.1

to be the necessary and sufficient observational conditions for the
Bs. Once these conditions are established, the theoretical task at
that level of generality is completed. The next stage in the development of science is to expand the framework at the next level of
generality by seeking another logical equivalency between a theory
and its assumptions and consequences.

21. The advocacy of logical equivalency as a research goal stems
from Samuelson's rejection of explanations in favour of descriptions
and from his reading of the history of science that the best-known
theories are descriptions, i.e. they are expressed (or can be expressed)
in the observational language of basic statements.

22. The activity of explaining or answering a 'why' question is
unscientific in Samuelson's opinion because it searches for the ultimate cause or explanation (see Samuelson, 1964, p. 737; 1965b,
pp. 102–3). It therefore lends support to the doctrine of '*a priorism*',
which Samuelson has attacked on many occasions (1964, p. 736;
see also 1947, p. 3; 1952, p. 62):

> Well, in connexion with the exaggerated claims that used to be
> made in economics for the power of deduction and *a priori*
> reasoning – by classical writers, by Carl Menger, by the 1932

Robbins . . . by the disciples of Frank Knight, by Ludwig von Mises – I tremble for the reputation of my subject.

For Samuelson the only viable alternative to *a priorism* is to ground theories in observations, i.e. to express theories in observational language. Thus we can understand why Samuelson dismisses Machlup's characterization that a theory is wider or transcends what is to be explained (see Machlup, 1964, p. 733; and Samuelson, 1964, p. 736).

23. Furthermore, argues Samuelson (1964, p. 737), scientists do not pursue explanations but, rather, descriptions of empirical reality:

> Scientists never 'explain' any behavior, by theory or by any other hook. Every description that is superseded by a 'deeper explanation' turns out upon careful examination to have been replaced by still another description, albeit possibly a more useful description that covers and illuminates a wider area.

The term 'explanation' as it is properly used in science is an honorific title for a better description, i.e. *'a better kind of description and not something that goes ultimately beyond description'* (Samuelson, 1965a, p. 1165; see also 1965b, p. 103). In this sense Samuelson believes that Newton's theory is a better description and not an explanation in comparison with its predecessor, Kepler's theory.

24. The stress on description of observable phenomena and the avoidance of metaphysics are the distinguishing features of the descriptivist position (see Passmore, 1966, ch. 14). Thus Nagel writes: 'the descriptive account of science was espoused by many thinkers who . . . sought to emancipate science from any dependence on unverifiable "metaphysical" commitments' (1961, p. 119).

25. Claiming the support of several physicists, Samuelson declares that the best-known theories in science are *'expressible completely* in terms of . . . "basic sentences" alone' (1965a, p. 1167; emphasis added). A basic sentence (statement) is of the form 'There exists an x with property P at place/time r/t' and it is used to describe an observable event. Hence a basic sentence (statement) is usually called an observational sentence.[4] Samuelson's examples of theories that are expressed solely in terms of basic sentences are the following: Galileo's theory of falling bodies; the Newtonian theory of gravitation as applied to the n-body problem; Einstein's special theory of

relativity; and the classical thermodynamics of Carnot, Clausius, Kelvin and pre-1900 Gibbs. These examples, in Samuelson's opinion, refute the contention of Massey that 'empirical science comes to maturity only after it effects a clean break with basic sentences, only after it boldly postulates theoretical statements that ultimately are anchored, though not submerged, in experience by means of semantic ties to basic sentences' (1965, p. 1163).[5]

26. The methodological constraint that a theory must be expressed solely in observational terms is also addressed to epistemological and metaphysical issues. The epistemological question 'What is knowledge?' is reduced to the methodological quest for the foundations of knowledge. Since for Samuelson the reliable source of knowledge is observation, (true) knowledge is that which can be derived from observations. Metaphysical matters are handled in a similar way. The question whether there exists entities which correspond to terms such as 'utility', 'preference', etc., is answered by permitting only observational terms in the theoretical schema. Thus non-observational (theoretical) terms which do not have observable counterparts do not appear in the observational equivalent of a theory.

27. It should be noted that in the 1950 interpretation Samuelson does not have any substantive objection to ordinal utility theory. Following an earlier paper (1938c) he does find wanting the lack of concern shown by economists in the task of deriving the empirical implications of ordinal utility theory. This opinion would not go undisputed by Hicks and Allen, or by Georgescu-Roegen. Many of the so-called empirical implications of ordinal utility theory in Samuelson (1938c) are found in earlier works, for example, in Hicks and Allen (1934) and Georgescu-Roegen (1936).

28. More interestingly, Samuelson now regards his earlier work (1938a) as an unsatisfactory solution to the problem of deriving the empirical implications of ordinal utility theory. The Samuelson Theory is only a necessary observational condition. What is needed are the necessary and sufficient observational conditions.

29. Therefore, our solution to the problem of understanding revealed preference theory as presented in Samuelson (1950b) is to show that, in Samuelson's opinion, the theory is a satisfactory solution to the problem of finding the observational equivalent of ordinal utility theory.

6.2 The Houthakker solution

1. In this section we outline Houthakker's proof of the logical equivalence of ordinal utility theory to revealed preference theory which is regarded by Samuelson as the solution to his problem of finding the observational equivalent of ordinal utility theory.

2. The point of departure in Houthakker (1950) is revealed preference theory (the Samuelson Theory), as formulated by Samuelson (1938a) and as later revised by Samuelson (1947, 1948). The Samuelson Theory, comments Houthakker, is useful in deriving a considerable part of ordinal utility theory but falls short of being the necessary and sufficient observational condition for ordinal utility theory, which, in his opinion, is and has been the problem of the revealed preference approach (see also Houthakker, 1961, p. 712).

3. Houthakker points out that revealed preference theory is a necessary but not a sufficient condition for ordinal utility theory because an 'anomalous' situation may occur. Consider the following account of consumer behaviour. Bundle X^0 is bought at price–income situation (P^0, I^0); X^1 at (P^1, I^1); X^2 at (P^2, I^2), such that $P^0X^0 \geq P^0X^1$ and $P^1X^1 \geq P^1X^2$. If the consumer is consistent, in the sense of the Samuelson Postulate, he will not be able to afford bundle X^0 at (P^1, I^1), or bundle X^1 at (P^2, I^2). However, he would not be inconsistent, in the sense of the Samuelson Postulate, if he can afford bundle X^0 at price–income situation (P^2, I^2), such that $P^2X^2 \geq P^2X^0$ and $P^0X^2 > P^0X^0$. In the terminology of revealed preference, bundle X^0 is revealed preferred to bundle X^1, bundle X^1 is revealed preferred to bundle X^2, bundle X^2 is revealed preferred to bundle X^0 and bundle X^0 is not revealed preferred to bundle X^2. By using revealed preference as a measure of preference, following Samuelson (1948),[6] it means that bundle X^0 is preferred to bundle X^1, bundle X^1 is preferred to bundle X^2 and bundle X^2 is preferred to bundle X^0; in other words, the consumer's preferences are inconsistent. This result is considered an anomaly because if preferences, measured in terms of revealed preference, are not consistent, then revealed preference theory is not logically equivalent to ordinal utility theory, in which preferences are said to be consistent.

4. The task for Houthakker, then, is to find within the framework of revealed preference the necessary and sufficient condition for ordinal utility theory (1950, p. 161, emphasis added):

The main object of our investigation is to find a proposition which, apart from continuity assumptions, summarises the entire theory of the standard case of consumer's behavior (no indivisible goods or choices between probabilities; all income spent). *Such a proposition should imply and be derivable from utility analysis; in other words, it should be a necessary and sufficient condition for the existence of ordinal utility.* Samuelson's hypothesis does not satisfy this criterion, being only a necessary condition and not a sufficient one, for although it can be derived from utility considerations it does not entail integrability, which is an essential property of utility functions.

5. The Houthakker solution is to reformulate the Samuelson Postulate:

If $P^0 X^0 \geq P^0 X^1$, then $P^1 X^0 > P^1 X^1$, where
X^t is bought at price–income situation
(P^t, I^t), $t = 0, 1$ (A)

as:

If $P^0 X^0 \geq P^0 X^1$, $P^1 X^1 \geq P^1 X^2, \ldots$,
$P^{t-1} X^{t-1} \geq P^{t-1} X^T$, then $P^T X^0 > P^T X^T$,
where X^t is bought at (P^t, I^t), $t = 1, 2$.
$\ldots$, $T-1$, T, and at least two bundles
are not identical.   (B)

In the terminology of revealed preference, the reformulated Samuelson Postulate reads:

If bundle X^0 is revealed preferred to bundle
X^1, bundle X^1 is revealed preferred to X^2,
$\ldots$, and bundle X^{T-1} is revealed preferred to
X^T, then X^T is not revealed preferred to X^0.

In Samuelson (1950b), it became known as the *strong axiom of revealed preference*; the Samuelson Postulate, the *weak axiom of revealed preference*. Using the 'strong axiom' and an adaptation of the procedure in Samuelson (1948) for the construction of an indifference curve, Houthakker shows that an indifference surface can be constructed from observations of market behaviour, provided there is an infinite number of bundles.

6. The innovative feature of the 'strong axiom' is that the revealed preference relation has the property of semi-transitivity,[7] the absence of which permits the occurrence of the anomaly in which the last

bundle of a revealed preference chain is revealed preferred to the first and not vice versa.[8] Clearly, the 'strong axiom' implies the 'weak axiom' but not vice versa. It is interesting to note that Houthakker derives the assumption that revealed preference is semi-transitive from a consideration of ordinal utility theory because in the latter theory preference (ordinal utility) is assumed to be transitive. Thus Houthakker considers the amendment to the 'weak axiom' as a simple task of tying up the loose ends: 'the problem of integrability [the possible occurrence of the anomaly] arises only because of an incomplete statement of assumptions' (1950, p. 173).

7. Therefore, by replacing the 'weak axiom' with the 'strong axiom', Houthakker concludes that revealed preference theory can be shown to be the observational equivalent of ordinal utility theory (1950, p. 173):[9]

> We have shown that a theory based on semi-transitive
> revealed preference entails the existence of ordinal utility, while
> the property of semi-transitivity itself was derived from utility
> consideration. The 'revealed preference' and 'utility function'
> (or 'indifference surface') approaches to the theory of
> consumer's behaviour are therefore formally the same.

8. Samuelson, for his part, accepts the Houthakker extension of the 'weak axiom' as a proper adjustment to revealed preference theory and promptly declares that the Houthakker proof of the logical equivalence of ordinal utility theory to revealed preference theory 'complete[s] the program begun a dozen years ago of arriving *at the full empirical implications for demand behaviour of the most general ordinal utility analysis*' (1950b, p. 369). This judgment is reiterated in a later paper on revealed preference theory (Samuelson, 1953, p. 1; see also pp. 2, 8):

> The complete logical equivalence of this approach [revealed
> preference theory] with the regular Pareto–Slutsky–Hicks–Arrow
> ordinal preference approach has essentially been established.
> So in principle there is nothing to choose between the
> formulations.

9. Furthermore, in Samuelson's writings on methodology, the Houthakker proof is frequently cited by Samuelson in support of his methodology of descriptivism, which we have described in section

6.1. According to descriptivism, ideally a theory should be logically equivalent to its consequences. Thus we can understand why the Houthakker proof of the logical equivalence of ordinal utility theory with revealed preference theory is regarded by Samuelson as a vindication of his methodology (1963, pp. 234–5, emphasis added; see also 1964, p. 738):

> Let *B* be maximizing ordinal utility (satisfying certain regularity conditions) subject to a budget constraint defined by given income and prices.
>
> Let *C* be the Weak and Strong Axioms of revealed preference, which are stated in testable form $\Sigma P_j Q_j$, price–quantity data . . .
>
> *It happens that C implies B as well as being implied by it.* It is nonsense to think that *C* could be realistic and *B* unrealistic, and nonsense to think that the unrealism of *B* could then arise and be irrelevant.

6.3 A critique of the methodology of Paul Samuelson

1. At the outset it should be pointed out that the criticism levelled in section 5.3 against the use of revealed preference (defined in terms of behaviour) as an operational definition of preference applies equally to the interpretation of revealed preference theory as the observational equivalent of ordinal utility theory. In this section we shall accept the Houthakker proof in order to examine Samuelson's methodological view that, ideally, a theory is logically equivalent to its empirical consequences and his interpretation of revealed preference theory as the observational equivalent of ordinal utility theory. It should be clear that the criticism of Samuelson's methodology is external to the (conjectured) problem-situation, and is therefore independent of the discussion in section 6.1 of the consistency of the Samuelson Programme.

2. The goal of logical equivalency, which requires a theory to be expressed solely in observational language, is methodological. Accordingly, in our reconstruction of the problem-situation of revealed preference theory as presented in Samuelson (1950b), the focus was on the methodological constraint. In addition, we explained in the previous section that Samuelson regards the Houthakker proof of the logical equivalency of ordinal utility theory to revealed preference theory, as revised, as the solution to the problem of finding the observational equivalent of ordinal utility theory.

3. Since our criticism of Samuelson's methodology involves the rejection of his idea of explanation and the adoption of an alternative one, we shall first give an account of our theory of explanation. Although the following account of our theory of explanation duplicates in many respects what is given in section 4.3, it is included here to ensure continuity in our criticism of Samuelson's 1950 interpretation of revealed preference and to preserve the independence of this criticism from that contained in chapters 4 and 5.

4. Our view considers a theory to be an explanation of whatever strikes us to be in need of explanation, whether it is an individual event or a regularity. This view of a theory is known in the philosophy of science as the 'hypothetico-deductive' or 'deductive-nomological' theory of explanation (see Popper, 1935, ch. 3; Nagel, 1961, chs 3, 5; Hempel, 1966, chs 5, 6; and Hanson, 1961, pp. 39–63). The formal structure of an explanation exhibits the following features:

(1) it is a logical deduction, in which the statement that describes what is to be explained (the *explicandum*) is the conclusion and the statements that form 'the explanation' (the *explicans*) serve as premises;

(2) the *explicans* contains at least one unrestricted universal statement;

(3) if the *explicandum* describes the occurrence of an individual event, the *explicans* contains initial conditions which are in the form of singular statements; and

(4) if the *explicandum* describes the occurrence of a regularity, the *explicans* contains initial conditions which are in the form of universal statements.

5. An important, if not the most important, requirement for a satisfactory explanation is that the *explicans* is independently criticizable, i.e. criticizable apart from the *explicandum*. Put simply there is evidence for (and/or against) the *explicans* which is different from that for (and/or against) the *explicandum*. The rationale for this requirement is our interest in the pursuit of true explanations and explanations of greater depth and content. This requirement, which we shall call the *independence condition*, is satisfied implicitly in the explanation of an individual event because the *explicandum* is only one of many possible *explicanda* of the same type which are derivable from the unrestricted universal statement(s) in conjunction with the appropriate initial conditions. Moreover, it is clear that the

explicandum in this circumstance is a singular statement and is, thus, not derivable from the universal statement(s) alone. Logic requires singular statements as additional premises and the initial conditions fulfil this function.

6. On the other hand, in the explanation of a regularity, there is the possibility that the independence condition is not met since both constituents of the explanation do not include any singular statements. In other words, the *explicans* may be logically equivalent to the *explicandum*, in which case the *explicans* is a restatement of the *explicandum*. The *explicans* tells us no more than what is stated in the *explicandum*. The independence condition rules out the possibility that the explanation is circular (Nagel, 1961, pp. 36–7):

> The requirement that the premises must not be equivalent to
> the explicandum is sufficient to eliminate many pseudo-
> explanations, in which the premises simply rebaptize the facts
> to be explained by coining new names for them.

Most philosophers are in agreement on this point (see Popper, 1935, ch. 3 and appendix *X; 1957b, pp. 24–6; 1972, p. 351; Hempel, 1966, pp. 30–2; and Braithwaite, 1953, ch. 3, especially p. 76).

7. The independence condition implies that the *explicans* is of a higher degree of generality or universality than the *explicandum*, in the sense that the unrestricted universal statement(s) in conjunction with different initial conditions entail(s) other *explicanda*. The phenomenon described by a particular *explicandum* is explained as an instance of a more general phenomenon which is described by the unrestricted universal statement(s) of the *explicans*.

8. An additional requirement for a satisfactory explanation is that the *explicans* is falsifiable, i.e. it conflicts with a basic statement which describes some logically possible event. This requirement follows from the impossibility of verifying the *explicans* since it contains at least one unrestricted universal statement, and from the view that a theory *qua* explanation asserts more, the more it forbids.[10]

9. It should be pointed out that as a matter of defining an explanation we do not require that a satisfactory explanation is known to be true, though we hope that it is. From the above discussion, it is clear that it is logically impossible to verify an unrestricted universal statement. Thus even if an explanation is true, we cannot prove the assertion.

10. In light of our theory of explanation, we shall now evaluate the assertions that the explanatory view aims at ultimate explanations and that the term 'explanation' as it is properly used in empirical science refers to a better description, on the basis of which Samuelson rejects the explanatory view of theories.

11. Explanations need not be ultimate. To think otherwise, as Samuelson does, is to confuse the explanatory view with the essentialist one. This confusion is evident in Samuelson's rejection of explanations and in his continual reference of an explanation as *the* explanation: 'After Newton had described "how", he did not waste time on the fruitless quest of "why?" ... Nor has anyone since Newton provided "the explanation" ' (1964, p. 737).

12. *Essentialism* asserts that science must seek ultimate explanations which are neither capable nor in need of further explanation. It maintains that a theory *qua* explanation goes behind the appearance of phenomena to reveal their underlying essence.[11]

13. According to our explanatory view of theories, a theory is a conjecture, one which may be corrected and, moreover, be further explained in terms of another theory of a higher degree of universality. It therefore rejects the proposition that science must aim at ultimate explanations. This position also rejects as dogmatic the search for the foundations of knowledge (see Lakatos, 1962; and Popper, 1963a, intro.). Moreover, it allows for the possibility that there can be more than one logically satisfactory explanation of any given event or regularity.

14. Thus the quest of 'why?' is not as fruitless as Samuelson insists. We can adhere to the idea that we try to give an explanation of whatever we so choose and give up the essentialist notion that explanations are ultimate in the sense that they are neither in need nor capable of being further explained.

15. It can be shown that an explanation is not just a better description. This can be accomplished through a rebuttal of Samuelson's claims (1964, p. 737) that Newton's theory is just a better description than Kepler's and that Kepler's three laws together are necessary and sufficient conditions for the truth of Newton's theory as applied to the so-called 'two-body problem' (Samuelson, 1965a, p. 1169).

16. Both of these claims are false. Although Kepler's theory is a good approximation to Newton's theory, the two theories are

logically incompatible. To deduce Kepler's theory from Newton's, even as an approximation, it is necessary to make certain assumptions that are either false or logically inconsistent with Newtonian theory.

17. To deduce Kepler's third law from Newtonian theory, we have to assume either that the mass of every planet is the same or that the mass of every planet is zero. Both assumptions are false. Moreover, the latter assumption of zero mass is logically inconsistent with Newtonian theory because a body with zero mass does not conform to the laws of motion. Therefore, Kepler's theory does not provide the necessary and sufficient conditions for Newton's theory (see Born, 1949, pp. 129–33; Popper, 1957b, p. 29 and *passim*; 1972, pp. 357–8; Duhem, 1906, pt II, ch. 6, sec. 4; and Goldstein, 1950, p. 80). This criticism is in addition to the usual one that there is mutual attraction between the planets, which, incidentally, cannot be ignored even in the so-called two-body problem unless one adopts the instrumentalist position that a theory is merely an instrument or tool for predictions.

18. Furthermore, in correcting Kepler's results, Newton sought to explain them as good approximations in terms of more fundamental laws, the 'laws of motion' and 'universal gravitation'. Clearly, it is only after Newton's theory was conjectured that we learn in what respects Kepler's theory is a good approximation. Thus Newton did not only produce a better description in the sense of just being more general than Kepler's theory, but he also introduced new ideas which are of a higher degree of generality than Kepler's. In addition, he not only corrected Kepler's theory but Galileo's too. There is also the mistaken view which considers Newton's theory to be logically equivalent to the conjunction of the theories of Galileo and Kepler. As Popper (1972, p. 358) observes, if it were the case, Newton's theory cannot be regarded as progressive since it is then a circular explanation. However, it is not the case since Galileo's theory, like Kepler's theory, is logically inconsistent with Newton's theory (see Popper, 1957b, pp. 29–33). Therefore, it is unfounded historically to say that an explanation is only a better description.

19. Samuelson has rightfully condemned *a priorism*, the view that all phenomena can be explained as consequences of self-evident first principles, the truth of which is independent of all possible experience. The only viable alternative that Samuelson thinks is

available is to adopt a descriptivist methodology, requiring a theory to be expressed in observational language. This alternative, however, encounters numerous difficulties.

20. First, consider Samuelson's reply to Massey that well-known scientific theories are to be expressed completely in terms of basic statements (sentences) which are considered observational.

21. Galileo's theory of falling bodies, one of Samuelson's examples, is not logically equivalent to a set of basic statements. As a theory, it includes at least one unrestricted universal statement of the form 'For all x, if x is P, then x is Q,' where no spatio-temporal location is specified. On the other hand, a basic statement is of the form 'There exists an x with property P at place/time r/t.' A theory cannot be logically equivalent to a set of observational statements because an unrestricted universal statement is not equivalent to a finite conjunction of (observational) basic statements. In particular, Galileo's theory does not apply only to a finite number of bodies but to all bodies.

22. Similarly, the ordinal utility theory of consumer behaviour is not to be expressed in terms of a finite conjunction of basic statements. Its domain is not restricted to any finite set of individuals or to a particular spatio-temporal location. It is therefore impossible to verify this explanation of consumer behaviour.[12]

23. Second, there does not exist an independent observational language in which one could ground theories and theoretical concepts. While one may accept the criticism that a theory is not equivalent to a finite conjunction of basic statements, one may still wish to maintain that a theory is observational in so far as it contains only observational terms, terms which denote observable entities. For example, the statement 'This is a glass of water' is said to be observational because the names 'glass' and 'water' are observational terms.

24. However, observational terms are theory-laden.[13] For example, the term 'glass' is a universal term and therefore does not correspond to any particular entity. Moreover, in the definition of the word, we make use of terms which refer to certain dispositional properties. But a dispositional term is not correlated with any unique sensory experience. Thus, to test whether a particular object is a glass, we check for the dispositional properties of a glass. Therefore, the word 'glass' refers to objects which display certain law-like behaviour. This implies that the observational statement

117

'This is a glass of water' transcends that experience which gave rise to the statement.[14]

25. To accept the view that all observational terms are theory-laden would be incompatible with the descriptivist position,[15] for the view that knowledge consists essentially of observational reports is irreconcilable with the view that all observational terms are theory-laden. If the informative part of a statement is the observational part, then we do not know what a statement is asserting unless we can separate the observational from the theoretical. But then we cannot do this.[16]

26. Drawing on our criticism of Samuelson's descriptivist methodology and of his mistaken view of explanations, we shall now examine the third interpretation of revealed preference theory, i.e. as the full empirical implications of ordinal utility theory.

27. Is ordinal utility theory (OUT) an explanation of revealed preference theory (RPT)? Given our theory of explanation, the answer is 'No'. If ordinal utility theory is logically equivalent to revealed preference theory, as Samuelson argues, then the explanation is unsatisfactory because it is circular, failing to meet the independence condition that the *explicans* can be criticized independently of the *explicandum*. The *explicans* (OUT) is merely a restatement of the *explicandum* (RPT). Clearly, the statement 'OUT explains RPT' tells us nothing more about consumer behaviour than the *explicandum* alone. Similarly, RPT is not an explanation of OUT. Moreover, this raises the question as to why Samuelson (1963) calls OUT 'a theory' and RPT 'the set of empirical consequences'. It seems that this distinction is arbitrary. It must be concluded that OUT and RPT are not two different theories; at best, they are two different ways of expressing the same set of ideas. This is Samuelson's position in light of the Houthakker proof (Samuelson, 1953, p. 1, emphasis added):

> The complete logical equivalence of this approach [revealed preference theory] with the regular Pareto–Slutsky–Hicks–Arrow ordinal preference approach has essentially been established. *So in principle there is nothing to choose between the formulations.*

But if there is nothing to be gained from choosing one theory rather than another, it must be asked: What is the problem to which the revealed preference theory is a proposed solution?

28. Let us now consider Samuelson's main contention that revealed preference theory is the observational equivalent of the non-observational ordinal utility theory. It is from this standpoint that he interprets the Houthakker proof as the completion of the Samuelson Programme. A variety of arguments are advanced and we shall consider each in turn.

29. First, it is argued that revealed preference theory is verifiable empirically. As we have pointed out at the beginning of this section, a theory is not verifiable for a logical reason; namely it contains at least one unrestricted universal statement. Moreover, we pointed out that this is the reason why ordinal utility theory is not verifiable empirically. With respect to revealed preference theory, both the 'weak' and 'strong' axioms of revealed preference are unrestricted universal statements. They apply not only to a finite number of acts of buying by a single individual or to a finite number of individuals but to all cases of consumer behaviour of all individuals. Therefore, revealed preference theory, as with ordinal utility theory, is not verifiable empirically. This conclusion can be reached in a different way. If RPT is logically equivalent to OUT, as Samuelson believes, then if OUT is not empirically verifiable then neither is RPT. Alternatively, if RPT is verifiable empirically then so is OUT. In the latter case, we must raise the question: What problem is solved by RPT and not by OUT?

30. Second, it may be admitted that RPT is not verifiable empirically but it may, nevertheless, be maintained that, unlike OUT, RPT contains only observational (non-theoretical) terms. This position is untenable because revealed preference theory is not stated in observational terms, as we have argued in section 5.3.

31. It is argued that RPT is less theoretical or more observational than OUT because its main concept, 'revealed preference', is observational while the terms 'preference' and 'utility' are not. This distinction is illusory (see section 5.3). Consider, for example, the definition of 'revealed preferred' in Samuelson (1950b, p. 370, emphasis added):

> If at the price and income of situation *A* you *could* have bought the goods actually bought at different point *B* and if you actually chose not to, then *A* is defined to be 'revealed to be better than' *B*.

Given this definition, 'revealed preferred' is not an observational term because we cannot verify that the consumer could have bought bundle *B*. The point is that we cannot prove that the consumer could have bought bundle *B* because it depends on the willingness of the seller(s) to exchange that combination of goods for money and on the belief of the buyer that he could buy that combination if he so chose to do. Neither the dispositions and expectations of the seller(s) nor those of the buyer are subject to empirical verification. Needless to say, usually we do assume (but we cannot prove) that the seller and the buyer have these dispositions and expectations.

32. Finally, there is a variant to the argument that revealed preference theory can be expressed completely in observational terms. It is sometimes said that the theory is expressed completely with the use of the observational terms 'price' and 'quantity'. This position cannot be sustained because observations are embedded in theories. Consider the statement 'The price of an orange is £1.00.' This statement cannot be verified with observations because it expresses a complex set of ideas which transcends observable experience. It expresses the willingness of the person who possesses oranges to exchange them for pounds at the rate of £1.00 per orange. It conveys to a potential buyer the information that if he were to present £1.00 to the person who holds oranges, he would receive in exchange one orange. More importantly, it predicts that a transaction will take place if the one who holds oranges is willing to sell and an individual is willing to buy and if the buyer believes that the seller is willing to sell at that rate.[17] Clearly, there is no observable experience which we can use to verify these dispositions and expectations. All this is evident from the fact that since the term 'price' is a universal term, it is defined in terms of dispositional properties and expectations and does not, therefore, correspond to any unique sensory experience. Needless to say, there does not exist any physical ('hard') object which is called 'price'. One would hardly wish to argue that written records of prices are the same things as prices.

33. Our criticism of the various arguments that are used to support the proposition that revealed preference theory is observational underscores our contention that observations are never pure; they are embedded in expectations, assumptions and theories, and therefore transcend so-called 'observable experiences'. Moreover, it suggests that the problem of distinguishing between theoretical and observational terms cannot be solved.

34. In the social sciences we have to take into consideration the

fact that a person holds theories (expectations) about other people's behaviour or potential behaviour. This adds another obstacle to those that are thrown up against the numerous attempts in the philosophy of the natural sciences to solve the problem of distinguishing between observational and theoretical terms. We are here referring to the problems generated by the existence of human knowledge (see Popper, 1968a, 1972).

35. We now summarize our criticism of the interpretation that the problem of the revealed preference approach is to find the observational equivalent of the non-observational ordinal utility theory and of the Houthakker solution to this problem. First, revealed preference theory, as revised by Houthakker, is not an explanation but a restatement of ordinal utility theory. Second, revealed preference theory is not verifiable empirically because it uses unrestricted universal statements. Third, it is not verifiable empirically because its key term, 'revealed preference', is not defined exclusively in observational terms, and does not therefore denote observable experience, and because the terms 'price' and 'quantity' are not pure observational terms. Fourth, it is puzzling how Samuelson can consider revealed preference theory to be the logical equivalent to ordinal utility theory and at the same time argue that the former theory is observational while the latter is not. Fifth, Samuelson's descriptivist methodology upon which the interpretation is founded is beset with numerous logical and epistemological difficulties, some of which appear to be insurmountable. Thus we conclude that revealed preference theory, as revised by Houthakker, is not the observational equivalent of ordinal utility theory, and is not therefore the solution to the problem of finding the observational equivalent of ordinal utility theory. It should be emphasized that we have accepted the Houthakker proof solely for the purpose of criticizing Samuelson's present interpretation of the revealed preference theory. In section 5.3 we have expressed serious reservations about the logical equivalence of the two theories, except by defining 'choice' as 'preference'.

Chapter 7

Epilogue

7.1 Rational reconstruction self-applied

1. In the preceding three chapters we presented an interpretative study of Paul Samuelson's contributions to the revealed preference approach in the theory of consumer behaviour. This study is not above criticism; it too can be the object of a critical study. Criticism can help to expose and eliminate errors in our understanding of the Samuelson Programme. Ideally, this criticism will be founded on an understanding of our study. Thus, in this chapter, we shall present a rational reconstruction of our study and outline a procedure whereby it can in turn be criticized. This application of the method of rational reconstruction to this new problem of understanding should be seen as a demonstration of the generality, self-consistency and richness of the method in the study of theoretical work. Moreover, the exercise should be regarded as a test of the method, emphasizing our view that all aspects, without exception, of a theoretical study can be objects of criticism.

2. What is the problem of our study? The aim is to understand Samuelson's contributions to the revealed preference approach as a consistent programme of research. This task is problematic because there is *prima facie* evidence of inconsistencies in some of Samuelson's contributions. The solution to this problem is to partition it into three separate problems of understanding: the problem of understanding revealed preference theory as presented in Samuelson (1938a); the problem of understanding revealed preference theory as presented in Samuelson (1948); and the problem of understanding revealed preference theory as presented in Samuelson (1950b). In each problem of understanding, the following propositions form

122

the major constraints. First, there is the epistemological view that knowledge is conjectural. Second, there is the methodological position that there is no authoritative source for the acquisition of knowledge. Third, the method of rational reconstruction is accepted as the solution to the general problem of understanding any theoretical work. Fourth, there is the requirement that a solution to the problem of understanding theoretical work should be consistent with the documentary evidence that is available in the literature. The solution to each problem of understanding is a conjecture of the problem to which revealed preference theory is a proposed solution and an explanation of why Samuelson regarded the solution to be satisfactory. On the basis of this understanding, we constructed a critique of each problem-situation and solution, using arguments which are both within and outside the problem-situation.

3. Before we proceed to reconstruct and criticize each individual problem-situation of understanding, we can suggest how our study can be criticized in general terms. First, it can be criticized on the grounds that there is no problem of understanding because there are no inconsistencies in Samuelson's contributions that lead to a problem of understanding. Second, it may be argued that the problem of understanding the Samuelson Programme cannot be solved because certain constraints are incompatible. Third, the major constraints can be examined. The epistemological or the methodological views may be rejected. The method of rational reconstruction may be shown to be an unsatisfactory solution to the problem of understanding any theoretical work. The general problem of understanding itself may be attacked.

4. The problem in chapter 4 was to understand revealed preference theory (the Samuelson Theory) as presented in Samuelson (1938a). The theory is seen as Samuelson's solution to the problem of deriving the main results of ordinal utility theory without the use of utility or any other non-observational concept. The problem arises because, in Samuelson's opinion, ordinal utility theory (OUT) is not verifiable empirically. Accordingly, it can be asked of the Samuelson Theory: Is it justifiable in terms of observations of market behaviour? Independently of this question of consistency, it is asked whether the Samuelson Theory is an explanation of consumer behaviour because explanation is an aim of OUT.

5. In light of this understanding of Samuelson (1938a), the Samuelson Theory is criticized on the following points:

(1) the Samuelson Theory is not verifiable by observations of market behaviour (section 4.3, para. 6);
(2) the Samuelson Theory is readily accepted because of an antecedent acceptance of OUT (section 4.3, para. 10);
(3) the Samuelson Theory is not an explanation of consumer behaviour (section 4.4, para. 4).

It is then concluded that the Samuelson Theory is not a satisfactory solution to the problem of deriving the main results of ordinal utility theory without the use of non-observational concepts, and, therefore, it is not a replacement for ordinal utility theory.

6. To refute criticism (1), it is necessary to show either (i) that OUT is not rejected because it is not verifiable empirically, or (ii) that the Samuelson Theory is verifiable by observations of market behaviour. In addition, the reasons why the Samuelson Theory is considered superior to OUT must be explained. Criticism (2) can be rejected by giving a self-consistent explanation for the ready acceptance of the Samuelson Theory. Criticism (3) can be rejected by showing either (i) that OUT is not an explanation of consumer behaviour, or (ii) that the idea of explanation is problematic, or (iii) that the 'explanation' of consumer behaviour that is constructed from the Samuelson Theory is unacceptable, for example it does not satisfy the idea of explanation.

7. The problem in Chapter 5 was to understand revealed preference theory as presented in Samuelson (1948). The theory is seen as Samuelson's solution to the problem of constructing an individual's indifference map from observations of his market behaviour. It is pointed out that this latter problem is considered by Samuelson as an extension of the theory which was presented in Samuelson (1938a). A major constraint of the 1948 problem-situation is operationalism, a doctrine designed to give empirical meaning to concepts in terms of observable and repeatable procedures.

8. The problem of revealed preference theory as presented in Samuelson (1948) is criticized on the following grounds:

(4a) the problem of constructing an individual's indifference map is inconsistent with the problem of deriving the main results of ordinal utility theory without the use of utility or any other non-observational concept (section 5.1, para. 4);
(4b) there is a change in the interpretation of the Samuelson

Theory – it is about preferences after all (section 5.1, para. 9);

(4c) revealed preference theory should be regarded as a solution to the problem of justifying OUT (section 5.1, para. 20);

(4d) revealed preference theory is not therefore a new theory (section 5.1, para. 20).

9. The construction of an indifference curve which can be seen as an attempt to define the concept of indifference in operational terms is unsatisfactory:

(5) it is improper to assume that preferences do not change (section 5.3, para. 9);

(6) the proposed set of operations to define 'indifference' cannot be executed (section 5.3, para. 11);

(7) alternatively, the set of operations that can be carried out leads to a proliferation of concepts of indifference which are of no theoretical value (section 5.3, para. 14);

(8) 'revealed preference' is not the operational definition of 'preference' because it makes use of theoretical assumptions which are not verifiable (section 5.3, para. 27);

(9) a refutation of the Samuelson Postulate does not imply that preferences are inconsistent but that OUT is false (section 5.3, para. 54).

Thus it is concluded that revealed preference theory as presented in Samuelson (1948) is not an operational method for the construction of an individual's indifference map.

10. Criticisms (4a)–(4d) can be refuted in two ways: show either (i) that the two problems are consistent, or (ii) that we have misunderstood the problem of Samuelson (1938a) and/or the problem of Samuelson (1948). In either case it is also necessary to deal with criticisms (1)–(3) against Samuelson (1938a) *and* criticisms (5)–(9) against Samuelson (1948). Criticisms (5)–(9) can either be (i) refuted directly, or (ii) refuted indirectly by attacking our understanding of the operationalist thesis.

11. The problem in chapter 6 was to understand revealed preference theory as presented in Samuelson (1950b). The theory is seen as Samuelson's solution to the problem of deriving the full empirical implications of OUT by which is meant the observational equivalent of OUT. The major constraint of this latter problem is identified as

the methodology of descriptivism, which, ideally, requires a theory to be logically equivalent to its set of empirical consequences. This requirement is based on a rigid distinction between theoretical (non-observational) and observational terms.

12. The problem of Samuelson (1950b) is criticized on the grounds of consistency:

(10) the problem of finding the observational equivalent of ordinal utility theory is incompatible with the problem of deriving the main results of ordinal utility theory without the use of utility or any other non-observational concepts (section 6.1, para. 4).

13. Furthermore, the methodology of descriptivism is beset with numerous difficulties:

(11) from a logical and a historical perspective, it is shown that a theory is not ideally logically equivalent to its empirical consequences (section 6.3, para. 21);

(12) the distinction between theoretical and observational terms, upon which the goal of logical equivalency is founded, cannot be maintained – all observational terms are theory-laden (section 6.3, para. 24).

In light of this criticism of descriptivism, it is argued that:

(13) OUT is not an explanation of revealed preference theory, or vice versa (section 6.3, para. 27);

(14) revealed preference theory is not verifiable empirically (section 6.3, para. 29);

(15) revealed preference theory does not contain observational terms only (section 6.3, para. 32).

Thus it is concluded that revealed preference theory is not the observational equivalent of ordinal utility theory.

14. To refute criticism (10), one must show either (i) that the two problems are consistent, or (ii) that we have misunderstood the problem of Samuelson (1938a) and/or the problem of Samuelson (1948). However, one needs also to address oneself to criticisms (1)–(3) of Samuelson (1938a) and to criticisms (11)–(15) of Samuelson (1950b).

15. Criticisms (11)–(15) can be refuted by criticizing our theory of explanation and by showing that there exist observational terms

126

which are not theory-laden. Alternatively, each critical point can be refuted directly.

7.2 Concluding remarks

1. The Samuelson Programme can be characterized as methodological. It was launched by Samuelson because ordinal utility theory was considered methodologically unsatisfactory, not because it was inadequate theoretically or empirically; it was not asserted that the Samuelson Theory (revealed preference theory) offered new theoretical insights into consumer behaviour.

2. We have attributed the failure of the Samuelson Programme, more specifically Samuelson's solutions to the three problems, to an underlying methodology. The inadequacy of the solutions is not due to their specific formulations or errors in mathematics and logic. Their failure lies in the conception of the problems themselves. In view of our criticism of the methodology, it is suggested that these problems cannot be solved. Thus it would be wishful thinking to nurture the hope that solutions to the Samuelson problems await an ingenious mathematical proof. The philosophical difficulties confronting the Samuelson Programme and, by implication, the entire revealed preference approach cannot be avoided. Any new (proposed) solution must deal with these difficulties first.

3. The failure of the Samuelson Programme is of profound significance for economics in general. The alleged success of the Samuelson Programme gave respectability to the methodology of descriptivism and the related doctrine of operationalism. In the light of our analysis the paradigmatic value of revealed preference theory is cast in considerable doubt. Thus its underlying methodology must be evaluated on its own.

4. But, as we have argued, descriptivism and operationalism are indefensible on logical and historical grounds. Observation is a weak base upon which to ground theories or to give empirical meaning to theoretical concepts. Observations alone are not informative. They must be interpreted; thus theories are required. A choice of theories to interpret observations must be made. One need not despair at this prospect. It is through conflict of different interpretations that the growth of new theories takes place.

5. The Samuelson Programme was an attempt to free the theory of consumer behaviour from philosophical issues which have been

the source of many unresolved controversies in economics. This goal was fostered by the hope that methodological problems can be solved in the same, seemingly decisive, manner as problems in logic and mathematics. Our study has shown that this hope has not been, or is unlikely to be, realized. It is indeed ironic that an unintended consequence of the Samuelson Programme is that the theory of consumer behaviour has become not less but more philosophical.

Notes

Chapter 1 Introduction

1 Alternative versions (with corrections) of the formal proof are due to Newman (1960a, 1960b), Uzawa (1960), Richter (1966) and Stigum (1973).

2 Cf. Newman (1965, p. 130), who suggests that the choice should depend on whether prices are given or are to be explained.

3 Even those who seek to revise the neo-classical theory of consumer behaviour accept the Houthakker result; see for example, the characteristics approach of Lancaster (1966).

4 This conclusion is questioned by Wong (1973), who argues that Samuelson's critique of Friedman's methodology is invalid because it follows from a basic misunderstanding of Friedman's instrumentalist methodology.

5 For example, the theory of capital was the scene of lively but bitter controversies for over twenty years (see Harcourt, 1972).

6 It should not be forgotton that the theory of consumer behaviour under the names 'utility theory' and 'value theory' was in past times the centre of much controversy (see Dobb, 1973; Schumpeter, 1954; Sweezy, 1934; Viner, 1925).

7 Little (1949, p. 95, n. 2), Houthakker (1950, p. 150) and Georgescu-Roegen (1954a, p. 125, n. 29 and n. 31) drew attention to some of these inconsistencies, but they did not explore further the significance of them for Samuelson's position.

8 Houthakker (1961, pp. 705–6) and Schumpeter (1954, IV, Appendix to ch. 7), two important commentators on the subject, are of this opinion. On the other hand, Myrdal (1932, ch. 4), writing before the advent of revealed preference, considered as a fruitless exercise the attempt by Fisher and others to purge the psychological content from subjective value theory and retain its formal structure.

9 This is the *raison d'être* of Slutsky's famous paper: 'if we wish to place economic science upon a solid basis, we must make it completely independent of psychological assumptions and philosophical hypotheses' (1915, p. 27).

10 This attitude can be attributed to a large extent to the hostile attacks on Cassel's theory of value by Wicksell (for example in Wicksell, 1919); see also Stigler (1950, pp. 390–1).

11 Arrow (1951, p. 16, n. 11; 1959, p. 121) is one of the few economists who considers the revealed preference approach to follow in the tradition of Cournot (1838) and Cassel (1918).

Notes

12 Cf. the remarks of Lindbeck (1970, p. 342), a member of the nominating committee: 'Generally speaking, Samuelson's basic achievement during recent decades is that more than anyone else, he has helped raise the general analytical and methodological level of central economic theory.'

Chapter 2 Understanding and criticism

1 Cf. Becker (1962, p. 1): 'everyone more or less agrees that rational behavior simply implies consistent maximization of a well-ordered function, such as a utility or profit function.'

2 This point of view is emphasized in a recent study (Hacking, 1975) on the importance of language in the history of philosophy.

3 The method of rational reconstruction is developed in Popper (1945, ch. 14; 1957a, sec. 31; 1968b, especially sec. 9). Applications and extensions of this method are found in Agassi (1963), Lakatos (1963–4, 1970, 1971), Jarvie (1964, 1972) and Watkins (1965).

4 Cf. the attitude of Samuelson towards Cassel's approach to the theory of consumer behaviour (see chapter 1 above).

5 The method of rational reconstruction is often confused with the method of understanding by subjective re-enactment (see Popper, 1968b, sec. 12).

6 The reduction of all explanations in the social sciences to psychological explanations is entailed by the metaphysical doctrine of 'psychologism' (see section 2.2).

7 These objects inhabit what Popper (1968a) calls 'World 3': physical states make up 'World 1'; and mental states make up 'World 2'.

8 This brief discussion of epistemology draws heavily on the ideas of Karl Popper (1963a, intro.; 1972, ch. 2).

9 Cf. Lakatos (1962, p. 158): 'a deductive system [is] a "*Euclidean theory*" if the propositions at the top (*axioms*) consist of perfectly well known terms (*primitive terms*) and if there are *infallible truth-value-injections* at this top of the truth-value *True*, which follows downward through the deductive channels of truth-transmission (proofs) and inundates the whole system'.

10 The terms 'instrumentalist' and 'descriptivist' are introduced in a discussion of the methodological views of Friedman and Samuelson in Wong (1973) (see also Nagel, 1961, pp. 117–40; Popper, 1956).

11 See, in particular, Samuelson's comments (1965a) on Massey (1965).

12 Georgescu-Roegen (1966, 1971) has frequently questioned the applicability of the methodology of the physical sciences to economics.

13 Even the critics of contemporary theory have not fared better. For example, Morgenstern (1972b, p. 699) diagnosed the ills of the discipline as a case of bad methodological practices. However, any soundness of that diagnosis is vitiated by the prescription that economists should imitate the practices of excellent natural scientists. In Morgenstern (1972a), the prescription is to follow the practices in physical sciences and mathematics of Newton, Hilbert, and von Neumann by axiomatizing economic theory.

14 The term 'metaphysics', as used here, is not equivalent to 'paradigm', as used by Kuhn (1962), except in a restricted sense. Out of Mastermann's catalogue of Kuhn's twenty-one different definitions of 'paradigm', our idea of metaphysics is similar to what Mastermann (1970, p. 65) identifies as a metaphysical paradigm: a set of beliefs, a myth, a successful metaphysical speculation, a standard, a new way of seeing, an organizing principle governing perception, a map, something which determines a large area of reality. Cf. the haunted-house doctrines of Watkins (1958, secs IV and V) and the 'hard-core' of

a research programme of Lakatos (1970) (see also Agassi, 1963, 1964; and Koyré, 1968).

15 For Popper (1935), metaphysical theories, unlike empirical theories, are unfalsifiable; in fact, he uses falsifiability as the demarcation criterion between metaphysics and empirical science. Agassi (1964) countenances the difficulty but not the impossibility of refuting a metaphysical theory.

16 For Jarvie (1964, ch. 1, especially pp. 14–15), it is the central problem of anthropology.

17 For a critical discussion of Mills's psychologism, see Popper (1945, ch. 14). An evaluation of the alternatives to psychologistic individualism is found in Agassi (1960); see also O'Neill (1973).

18 Cf. Schlesinger's argument (1963, ch. 2) that the principle of micro reduction is founded on a confusion between physical or causal order and logical order. Therefore, psychologistic individualism cannot be justified by an appeal to the causal relationship between human minds and social entities.

19 Edgeworth (1881) introduced the concept of 'indifference' to economics, but not as an alternative to cardinal utility; cf. Shackle (1967, p. 9).

20 Cf. Robbins (1935, p. 89): 'It follows, then, that if we are to do our job as economists, if we are to provide a sufficient explanation of matters which every definition of our subject-matter necessarily covers, we must include psychological elements. They cannot be left out if our explanation is to be adequate.'

21 The reason for not identifying GET to be regulated by psychologistic individualism is that in some formulations, for example Cassel (1918), psychological assumptions are eschewed.

22 The reswitching controversy in the contemporary theory of capital attests to the legacy of the difference in the metaphysics of the two schools of thought (cf. Dobb, 1973, especially chs 1 and 9; and Harcourt, 1972, ch. 4).

23 Sen (1969) takes this option and proposes a social decision function (SDF), which differs with the SWF over the property of transitivity' (see also Sen, 1970, ch. 6).

24 In the opinion of Popper (1963a), criticism is indispensable to the empirical sciences. In fact, he characterizes the method of the empirical sciences as the method of conjecture and refutation.

25 Cf. Popper (1945, addendum to vol. 2 of the 1962 edn) on the difference between 'immanent' and 'transcendent' criticism.

26 See, for example, Harcourt's observation (1972, p. 119) that, outside the two Cambridges, the recent controversies in capital theory are regarded as 'silly'.

Chapter 3 The Hicks and Allen Programme

1 Other objections are directed at the formulations of such Austrian economists, such as Weiser, Mayer and Strigl, who were all mentioned in Sweezy (1934), a paper to which Samuelson (1938c, 1947) has made reference. However, no reference to Sweezy's paper or to these economists appears in Samuelson (1938a).

2 Two additional objections are made in later writings. In Hicks (1939, p. 32) it is argued that the advantage of the Hicks–Allen theory is that it can deal with the income effects of a price change (see also Shackle, 1967, pp. 85–6). In Hicks (1956, ch. 2) the assumption of independent utility is explicitly rejected.

3 The acceptance of individualism does not entail any commitment to psychologism (see Popper, 1945, ch. 14).

131

4 Pareto, who also had an important influence on Hicks and Allen, is less equivocal than Marshall on psychologism: 'La psychologie est évidemment à la base de l'économie politique et, en général, de toutes les sciences sociales. Un jour viendra peut-être où nous pourrons déduire des principes de la psychologie les lois de la science sociale' (1909, p. 40).

5 The abandonment of the doctrine of psychologism through the recognition that preferences can be influenced and formed by conditions external to an individual calls for a re-examination of the role played by the concept of preference in economic theory.

6 This term is due to Lakatos (1970, p. 134 and *passim*).

7 In Hicks's most recent writing on consumer theory (1956, especially ch. 2), the emphasis remains on the irrelevance of a measurable concept of utility.

8 Such a reconsideration, it seems, should involve an enquiry into the proper use of 'Occam's razor' in theoretical studies.

9 Cf. Robinson (1962, p. 47): '*Utility* is a metaphysical concept of impregnable circularity, *utility* is the quality in commodities that makes individuals want to buy them, the fact that individuals want to buy commodities shows that they have *utility*.'

10 In Hicks and Allen (1934), the name 'Principle of Increasing Marginal Rate of Substitution' is used. Hicks (1939, p. 20, n. 1) changes the name to conform with the terminology of Marshall's theory.

11 Whether or not indifference curves with flat portions are more realistic is not the issue.

12 The 'Buridan's ass' metaphor is more applicable, it seems, to the choice situation of the theorist rather than that of the consumer.

13 Viner (1925) supports utility theory against its critics with the defence that the theory does explain the law of demand.

14 In Samuelson (1953), the fact that the law of demand is not derivable from revealed preference theory is considered a virtue.

15 Stigler seems to say that what is important is that the intended logical consequences, i.e. downward-sloping demand curves, are derivable in ordinal utility theory. This suggests that he has an instrumentalist view of theories (see Wong, 1973).

16 With few exceptions, most economists identify those goods with upward-sloping demand curves as Giffen goods (see, for example, Samuelson, 1953, pp. 1–2; Henderson and Quandt, 1971; and Lipsey and Rosenbluth, 1971).

17 This argument draws heavily on Vandermeulen (1972), in which it is argued that Giffen goods are not likely to have upward-sloping demand curves and that growing affluence rather than poverty is more likely to account for upward-sloping demand curves.

18 After reviewing the case for Giffen goods, especially the correspondence between Marshall and Edgeworth, Stigler (1947) finds Marshall's explanation of the Giffen good unconvincing.

19 This is the approach of Lipsey and Rosenbluth (1971); but the implications of this option for the rest of economics need not be considered.

Chapter 4 A new theory

1 The commensurability of scientific theories is a subject which has generated much lively debate among contemporary historians and philosophers of science (see Feyerabend, 1975; Kuhn, 1962; Lakatos and Musgrave, 1970; Lakatos, 1971; Popper, 1957b).

2 In chapter 5 we shall argue that calling the new theory 'revealed preference

theory' is a significant change in Samuelson's interpretation of the purpose of his theory.

3 Houthakker (1950) notes that although Samuelson originally regarded his new approach as a substitute for ordinal utility theory, he later (1947) considered it as a complement (see section 6.1).

4 The title of this paper, 'The Empirical Implications of Utility Analysis', suggests that Samuelson never intended to devise a new theory. However, in reference to his first paper (1938a) he wrote: 'There I expressed my opinion as to the *advantages from a methodological point of view of such a reorientation. Completely without prejudice to such considerations* I should like here to indicate the mathematical simplicities which suggest themselves from that investigation' (1938c, p. 346; emphasis added).

5 Various criticisms against utility theory are chronicled and assessed in Viner (1925).

6 This difference is evident in the empirical research generated by the two theories. For example, MacCrimmon and Toda (1969), who follow Hicks and Allen, try to construct an individual's indifference map based on data from controlled experiments, while Koo (1963, 1971) and Koo and Hasenkamp (1972), who follow Samuelson, work only with market data.

7 The idea that we must justify our knowledge (theories) has played an important role in shaping the nature and direction of philosophical enquiry (see Popper, 1963a, ch. 1; 1972, chs 1 and 2, especially sec. 21; and Bartley, 1964).

8 We coin a new term for the same reason that we use the term 'Samuelson Theory' – we argue in chapter 5 that using the term 'revealed preference theory' signals a change in Samuelson's interpretation of his theory.

9 In Samuelson (1938a) only the negative semi-definiteness of the substitution matrix is identified as a major result of ordinal utility theory, but in the addendum to the original paper (Samuelson, 1938b) it is also shown that the single-valuedness and homogeneity conditions are derivable from the Samuelson Postulate (in conjunction with auxiliary propositions).

10 The necessity of justifying knowledge, which is often considered as the hallmark of rationality, has been subjected to penetrating criticism by Popper (see especially 1972, chs 1 and 2). Bartley (1964) takes up Popper's attack on justificationist philosophers. He assesses critically various theories of rationality and proposes a non-justificationist solution to the problem of rationality; see also Agassi (1969).

11 This trivial interpretation is used by Houthakker to interpret a 'violation' of the postulate as an indication of a change of tastes: 'The axioms refer to a single individual at one instant of time' (1961, p. 713). Since we are arguing that the postulate as formulated in Samuelson (1938a) is not about preferences, we shall defer discussion of Houthakker's point to chapter 5.

12 Cf. Sen (1971, p. 312): 'Are the rationality axioms to be used only after establishing them to be true?'

13 This criticism also applies to the assumptions of given demand functions and that all income is spent in each buying situation.

14 Cf. Batra and Pattanaik (1972), whose main concern is to find the weakest formulation of the 'weak axiom' from which to derive the 'demand theorem'. This kind of exercise, which is pervasive in economics, raises the question of why we are interested in using weak assumptions. A satisfactory answer will have to distinguish between whether we are interested in explanations or prescriptions of behaviour.

15 Other writers have also expressed doubt about the alleged independence of

the Samuelson Theory from ordinal utility theory (see, for example, Georgescu-Roegen, 1954a, p. 125; Stigler, 1966, p. 68; Boland, 1971, p. 106).

16 Instead, Sen employed the criticism that the postulate is not verifiable empirically to advocate, following Arrow (1959) and Sen (1971, pp. 311–12), that the restriction of the domain of the 'weak axiom' to budget sets only should be relaxed to include all finite subsets. This proposal, argued Sen, makes the so-called 'strong axiom' redundant since intransitivity, which is ruled out by the 'strong axiom' but not by the original formualtion of the 'weak axiom', is a violation of the amended 'weak axiom'. Without any inconsistency, one can apply Sen's argument to dispense with revealed preference axioms altogether so as to use preference axioms only.

17 Samuelson has disavowed any interest in explanation and, moreover, has denied the possibility of explaining apart from describing. This methodological stance is evaluated in chapter 6.

18 This discussion of 'explanation' relies on Popper (1957b; 1972, appendix).

19 This kind of incomplete explanation Hempel calls 'partial explanations'. Thus he writes: 'I think it is important, . . . from what might be called *deductively complete explanations*, i.e., those in which the explanandum as stated is logically implied by the explanans; for the latter do, whereas the former do not, account for the explanandum phenomenon in the specificity with which the explanandum sentence describes it' (1965, pp. 416–17). This sense of completeness is also discussed in Boland (1970b).

20 Cf. the remarks on the difference between element-valued choice functions and set-valued choice functions in Sen (1971).

21 This *ad hoc* stratagem, which reduces the explanatory content of a theory, is an example of what is known in the literature of the philosophy of science as 'degenerating problem-shift' (see Lakatos, 1970, p. 118).

Chapter 5 A method of revealing preferences

1 Little detected this inconsistency in the 1947 problem of constructing an indifference curve: 'Although Professor Samuelson does indicate that an indifference curve may be traced out by the above method, the whole of his discussion implies that *this would only be a tracing out of what is already known*' (1949, p. 95; emphasis added). See also Houthakker (1950, p. 159) and Georgescu-Roegen (1954a, p. 125, n. 29 and n. 31). We have argued that this problem does not belong to the research programme launched in Samuelson (1938a).

2 In a well-known paper on the measurement of real national income, Samuelson (1950a) makes the same inference that an observed equilibrium bundle is preferred to all bundles which cost no more. He assumes explicitly that these other bundles lie on a lower indifference curve. In other words, the exercise is conducted within the context of ordinal utility theory.

3 Samuelson uses the term 'revealed inferior' to state this conclusion. Thus 'X^0 is revealed preferred to X^1' and 'X^1 is revealed inferior to X^0' are two definitionally equivalent statements describing the same observed relation between two bundles: X^0 is bought and X^1 did not cost more (cf. Samuelson, 1947, p. 152; and Baumol, 1972, pp. 221–6).

4 This methodological goal of stability in science is emphasized by Bridgman: 'We should now make it our business to understand so thoroughly the character of our permanent mental relations to nature that another change in our attitude, such as that due to Einstein, shall be forever impossible. It was perhaps excusable that a revolution in mental attitude should occur once . . .

but it would certainly be a reproach if such a resolution should ever prove necessary again' (1927, p. 2; emphasis added).

5 Operational analysis also pertains to what Bridgman (1927, p. 5) calls 'mental concepts', for example mathematical concepts. We are concerned here with only those concepts which are particular to empirical science and to the purpose of operationally defining them (cf. Hempel, 1965, p. 124).

6 For example, the concept of 'temperature' which is measured by an alcohol thermometer is distinguished from the concept of temperature which is measured by a mercury thermometer (see Hempel, 1966, pp. 92–3).

7 Cf. Little (1949, p. 92): 'The trouble with "indifference", as with "preference" . . . is that it is a subjective concept. There is certainly no obvious kind of market behaviour which can be called indifferent. How long must a person dither before he is pronounced indifferent?'

8 Cf. Sraffa's remarks on the measurement of capital (Hague, 1963, pp. 305–6), i.e. that in theoretical measurement, in contrast to statistical measurement, absolute precision is necessary.

9 Our criticism of operationalism draws on Popper (1935, pp. 439–40; 1963a, p. 62; 1963b, pp. 210–12) and Gillies (1972, pp. 5–8, 23; 1973, pt 1).

10 This is similar to Little's attempt (1949) to explain behaviour in terms of consistency of behaviour (see section 4.4).

11 Cf. Samuelson on the *interpretation* of apparently inconsistent choices as a situation of indifference: 'If our preference field does not have simple concavity – and why should it? – we may observe cases where A is preferred to B at some times, and B to A at others. If this is a pattern of consistency and not of chaos, we would choose to regard A and B as "indifferent" under those circumstances. If the preference field has simple concavity "indifference" will never explicitly reveal itself to us except as the results of an infinite limiting process' (1948, p. 248, n. 1). It should be noted that in the cited passage 'preferred' is synonymous with 'revealed preferred'. Otherwise, what does it mean to observe a preference?

12 Cf. Majumdar (1958), who observes that behaviour may not reveal preference in a gaming situation.

13 Cf. Popper (1963a, p. 62): '*measurements presuppose theories.* There is no measurement without a theory and no operation which can be satisfactorily described in non-theoretical terms. The attempts to do so are always circular; for example, the description of the measurement of length needs a (rudimentary) theory of heat and temperature-measurement; but these, in turn, involve measurements of length.'

14 Cf. Quine (1951, p. 41; see also pp. 42–6): 'our statements about the external world face the tribunal of sense experience not individually but only as a corporate body' (see also Lakatos, 1970, appendix; Wong, 1973, p. 318).

15 The fact that the consumer did not buy the bundle that ordinal utility theory predicts has nothing to do with whether or not the consumer is telling the truth about his preferences; see Murakami (1968, pp. 3–4), who regards an individual's decision to be *equivalent* to his preference.

16 This is the substance of Mossin's criticism (1972, pp. 183–4) of Koo's test (1963) of revealed preference theory.

Chapter 6 The observational equivalent of ordinal utility theory

1 One of the most influential proponents of the descriptivist (or descriptive) position was Ernst Mach, the physicist. On a number of occasions, Samuelson (1965a, 1972) acknowledged his debt to Mach's views on science.

Notes

2 Samuelson does not seem to be aware of the so-called 'paradoxes of confirmation' (see Goodman, 1955; and Watkins, 1957, 1960).

3 The symbol ⊃ is ambiguously used by Samuelson. It is not clear whether it signifies class inclusion or implication.

4 The term 'basic sentence' is introduced by Massey (1965, p. 1160) in his criticism of Samuelson's methodology (cf. Popper, 1935, sec. 28).

5 Much of the confusion evident in the exchange between Samuelson and Massey can be attributed to Massey's rather uncritical use of the term 'basic sentence'. Massey considers those sentences which are basic to be properly called 'true' or 'false'. Theoretical sentences on this view cannot be called 'true' or 'false'; their acceptance is only indirectly linked with observable experience. To draw such a distinction between theoretical and basic sentences, Massey has adopted the view that basic sentences are the fundamental and thus indisputable building blocks of scientific theories. This view overlooks the theoretical content of basic sentences and thus the implication that theoretical sentences can also be true or false (see section 6.3).

6 Throughout Houthakker (1950) it is assumed that behaviour (revealed preference) is a measure of preference. Therefore, our criticisms in section 5.3 against treating revealed preference as a measure of preference apply equally to Houthakker's analysis. This suggests a consideration of the so-called 'integrability problem' is warranted.

7 Semi-transitivity is a logically weaker property than transitivity. It should be noted that in Samuelson (1948) transitivity of revealed preference is assumed. This assumption allows Samuelson, for example, to infer that some bundle A is revealed preferred to any Cauchy–Lipschitz approximation to the indifferent bundle B (see section 5.3; and Baumol, 1972, p. 225, n. 16).

8 Sen (1971) has shown that the 'weak axiom' implies the 'strong axiom' if its domain includes all finite subsets.

9 Houthakker's proof is corrected by Corlett and Newman (1952–3), who stress the importance of the transitivity assumption in the proof. Alternative versions (with corrections) are due to Newman (1960a, 1960b), Uzawa (1960), Richter (1966) and Stigum (1973); see also Ville (1946).

10 The criterion of falsifiability is at the heart of Popper's negativist epistemology (see Popper, 1935, ch. 1, sec. 6, and ch. 5).

11 The essentialist and instrumentalist views of theories are contrasted with the explanatory one in Popper (1956).

12 Cf. Popper (1935, p. 63): 'For the verification of a natural law could only be carried out by empirically ascertaining every single event to which the law might apply, and by finding that every such event actually conforms to the law – clearly an impossible task.'

13 The expression 'theory-laden' is due to Hanson (1968). The thesis that observations are theory-laden is an important part of Popper's view that knowledge is conjectural (see Popper, 1972, ch. 1). The doctrine that there exists a pure observational language in which to ground theories is criticized in Nagel (1961, pp. 117–29).

14 Our criticism relies on Popper (1935, pp. 93–5 and Appendix *X; 1956, pp. 118–19). Popper (1972, ch. 2, sec. 18) also argues that theories are built into our sense organs.

15 This is similar to our criticism in section 5.3 of the operationalist thesis (see Popper, 1935, p. 440; 1963b, pp. 210–12), who argues that operational definitions are circular.

16 The preceding argument, which is based on the criticism of sensationalism in Agassi (1966), suggests that the problem of distinguishing between the

observational and the theoretical cannot be solved, and that theoretical issues in economics which are founded on this distinction should be reconsidered.

17 The point that predictions are implicit in observational terms is expressed very clearly in Agassi (1966, p. 13), who develops further the idea of Popper that all observations are theory-laden.

Bibliography

Afriat, S. N. (1967) 'The Construction of Utility Functions from Expenditure Data', *International Economic Review*, vol. 8, pp. 67–77.

Agassi, J. (1960) 'Methodological Individualism', *British Journal of Sociology*, vol. 11, pp. 244–70.

— (1963) 'Towards a Historiography of Science', *History and Theory*, no. 2.

— (1964) 'The Nature of Scientific Problems and Their Roots in Metaphysics', in M. Bunge, ed., *The Critical Approach to Science and Philosophy*, New York: Free Press, pp. 189–211.

— (1966) 'Sensationalism', *Mind*, vol. 75, pp. 1–24.

— (1969) 'Unity and Diversity in Science', in R. S. Cohen and M. W. Wartofsky, eds, *Boston Studies in the Philosophy of Science*, vol. 4, Dordrecht: Reidel, pp. 463–522.

Allen, R. G. D. (1938) *Mathematical Analysis for Economists*, London: Macmillan.

Arrow, K. J. (1951) *Social Choice and Individual Values*, New York: Wiley, 2nd ed., 1963.

— (1959 'Rational Choice Functions and Orderings', *Economica*, vol. 26, pp. 121–7.

— (1967) 'Samuelson Collected', *Journal of Political Economy*, vol. 75, pp. 730–7.

Bartley, W. W. (1964) 'Rationality versus the Theory of Rationality', in M. Bunge, ed., *The Critical Approach to Science and Philosophy*, New York: Free Press, pp. 3–31.

Batra, R. N. and Pattanaik, P. K. (1972) 'A Note on the Derivation of the Demand Theorem in the Revealed Preference Approach', *Economic Journal*, vol. 82, pp. 205–9.

Baumol, W. J. (1972) *Economic Theory and Operations Analysis*, 3rd ed., Englewood Cliffs, N.J.: Prentice-Hall.

Becker, G. S. (1962) 'Irrational Behavior and Economic Theory', *Journal of Political Economy*, vol. 70, pp. 1–13.

Boland, L. A. (1970a) 'Conventionalism and Economic Theory', *Philosophy of Science*, vol. 37, pp. 239–48.

— (1970b) 'Axiomatic Analysis and Economic Understanding', *Australian Economic Papers*, vol. 9, pp. 62–75.

— (1971) 'Methodology as an Exercise in Economic Analysis', *Philosophy of Science*, vol. 38, pp. 105–17.

138

Born, M. (1949) *Natural Philosophy of Cause and Chance*, Oxford: Clarendon Press.

Boulding, K. E. (1939) 'Review of J. R. Hicks, *Value and Capital*', *Canadian Journal of Economics and Political Science*, vol. 5, pp. 521–8.

Braithwaite, R. B. (1953) *Scientific Explanation*, Cambridge University Press.

Bridgman, P. W. (1927) *The Logic of Modern Physics*, New York: Macmillan.

Brown, A. and Deaton, A. (1972) 'Models of Consumer Behavior: A Survey', *Economic Journal*, vol. 82, pp. 1145–1236.

Cassel, G. (1918) *Theoretische Sozialökonomie*, Leipzig: Scholl; translated by J. MacCabe as *The Theory of Social Economy*, 2 vols, London: Unwin, 1923.

Chipman, J. S., Hurwicz, L., Richter, M. K. and Sonnenschein, H. F., eds (1971) *Preferences, Utility, and Demand*, New York: Harcourt Brace Jovanovich.

Corlett, W. J. and Newman, P. K. (1952–3) 'A Note on Revealed Preference and the Transitivity Condition', *Review of Economic Studies*, vol. 20, pp. 156–8.

Cournot, A. (1838) *Recherches sur les principes mathématiques de la théorie des richesses*, Paris: Hachette; translated by N. T. Bacon as *Researches into the Mathematical Principles of the Theory of Wealth*, London: Macmillan, 1897.

Debreu, G. (1954) 'Representation of a Preference Ordering by a Numerical Function', in R. M. Thrall, C. H. Coombs and R. L. Davis, eds, *Decision Processes*, New York: Wiley, pp. 159–65.

Diewert, W. E. (1973) 'Afriat and Revealed Preference', *Review of Economic Studies*, vol. 40, pp. 419–25.

Dobb, M. H. (1973) *Theories of Value and Distribution since Adam Smith*, Cambridge University Press.

Duhem, P. (1906) *La Théorie physique: son objet, sa structure*, Paris: Chevalier et Rivière; translated by P. P. Wiener from 2nd ed. (1914) as *The Aim and Structure of Physical Theory*, Princeton University Press, 1954.

Edgeworth, F. Y. (1881) *Mathematical Psychics*, London: Kegan Paul.

Ekelund, R. B., Jr., Furubotn, E. G. and Gramm, W. P. (1972) *The Evolution and State of Modern Demand Theory*, Lexington, Mass.: Heath.

Ferguson, C. E. (1972) *Microeconomic Theory*, 3rd ed., Homewood, Ill.: Irwin.

Feyerabend, P. K. (1975) *Against Method*, London: New Left Books.

Fisher, I. (1892) 'Mathematical Investigations in the Theory of Values and Prices', *Transactions of the Connecticut Academy of Arts and Sciences*, vol. 9, pp. 1–124.

Friedman, M. (1953) 'The Methodology of Positive Economics', *Essays in Positive Economics*, Chicago University Press, pp. 3–43.

Gale, D. (1960) 'A Note on Revealed Preference', *Economica*, vol. 27, pp. 348–54.

Georgescu-Roegen, N. (1936) 'The Pure Theory of Consumer's Behavior', *Quarterly Journal of Economics*, vol. 50, pp. 545–93.

— (1954a) 'Choice and Revealed Preference', *Southern Economic Journal*, vol. 21, pp. 119–30.

— (1954b) 'Choice, Expectations, and Measurability', *Quarterly Journal of Economics*, vol. 48, pp. 503–34.

— (1966) *Analytical Economics: Issues and Problems*, Harvard University Press.

— (1968) 'Utility', in *International Encyclopedia of the Social Sciences*, New York: Free Press, vol. 16, pp. 236–67.

— (1971) *The Entropy Law and the Economic Process*, Harvard University Press.

— (1973) 'Review of Chipman *et al.*, eds, *Preferences, Utility, and Demand*', *Journal of Economic Literature*, vol. 11, pp. 528–32.

Gillies, D. A. (1972) 'Operationalism', *Synthese*, vol. 25, pp. 1–24.

— (1973) *An Objective Theory of Probability*, London: Methuen.

Goldstein, H. (1950) *Classical Mechanics*, Reading, Mass.: Addison-Wesley.

Bibliography

Goodman, N. (1955) *Fact, Fiction, and Forecast*, Harvard University Press.

Green, H. A. J. (1971) *Consumer Theory*, Harmondsworth: Penguin (rev. ed., London: Macmillan, 1976).

Hacking, I. (1975) *Why Does Language Matter to Philosophy?* Cambridge University Press.

Hague, D. C. (1963) 'Summary Record of the Debate', in F. A. Lutz and D. C. Hague, eds, *The Theory of Capital*, London: Macmillan, pp. 289–403.

Hahn, F. H. (1973) 'The Winter of our Discontent', *Economica*, vol. 40, pp. 322–30.

Haley, B. F. (1939) 'Review of J. R. Hicks, *Value and Capital*', *American Economic Review*, vol. 29, pp. 557–60.

Hanson, N. R. (1968) *Patterns of Discovery*, Cambridge University Press.

— (1972) *Observation and Explanation*, London: Allen & Unwin.

Harcourt, G. C. (1972) *Some Cambridge Controversies in the Theory of Capital*, Cambridge University Press.

Harrod, R. F. (1939) 'Review of J. R. Hicks, *Value and Capital*', *Economic Journal*, vol. 49, pp. 294–300.

Hempel, C. G. (1965) *Aspects of Scientific Explanation*, New York: Free Press.

— (1966) *Philosophy of Natural Science*, Englewood Cliffs, N.J.: Prentice-Hall.

Henderson, J. M. and Quandt, R. E. (1971) *Microeconomic Theory*, 2nd ed., New York: McGraw-Hill.

Herzberger, H. G. (1973) 'Ordinal Preference and Rational Choice', *Econometrica*, vol. 41, pp. 187–237.

Hicks, J. R. (1939) *Value and Capital*, Oxford: Clarendon Press; 2nd ed., 1946.

— (1956) *A Revision of Demand Theory*, Oxford: Clarendon Press.

— (1974) 'Preference and Welfare', in A. Mitra, ed., *Economic Theory and Planning*, Calcutta: Oxford University Press, pp. 3–16.

— and Allen, R. G. D. (1934) 'A Reconsideration of the Theory of Value', *Economica*, vol. 1, pp. 52–76, 196–219.

Houthakker, H. S. (1950) 'Revealed Preference and the Utility Function', *Economica*, vol. 17, pp. 159–74.

— (1961) 'The Present State of Consumption Theory', *Econometrica*, vol. 29, pp. 704–40.

— (1965) 'On the Logic of Preference and Choice', in A. T. Tymieniecka, ed., *Contributions to Logic and Methodology in Honor of J. M. Bochenski*, Amsterdam: North-Holland, pp. 193–207.

Jarvie, I. C. (1964) *The Revolution in Anthropology*, London: Routledge & Kegan Paul.

— (1972) *Concepts and Society*, London: Routledge & Kegan Paul.

Jevons, W. S. (1871) *The Theory of Political Economy*, London: Macmillan; 4th ed., 1911, Penguin reprint, 1970.

Katzner, D. W. (1970) *Static Demand Theory*, New York: Macmillan.

Kihlstrom, R., Mas-Colell, A. and Sonnenschein, H. (1976) 'The Demand Theory of the Weak Axiom of Revealed Preference', *Econometrica*, vol. 44, pp. 971–978.

Koo, A. Y. C. (1963) 'An Empirical Test of Revealed Preference Theory', *Econometrica*, vol. 31, pp. 646–64.

— (1971) 'Revealed Preference – A Structural Analysis', *Econometrica*, vol. 39, pp. 89–97.

— and Hasenkamp, G. (1972) 'Structure of Revealed Preference: Some Preliminary Evidence', *Journal of Political Economy*, vol. 80, pp. 724–44.

Kornai, J. (1971) *Anti-Equilibrium*, Amsterdam: North-Holland.

Koyré, A. (1968) *Metaphysics and Measurement*, London: Chapman & Hall.

Kuhn, T. S. (1962) *The Structure of Scientific Revolutions*, Chicago University Press; 2nd ed., 1970.

Lakatos, I. (1962) 'Infinite Regress and the Foundations of Mathematics', *Aristotelian Society Supplementary Volume*, vol. 36, pp. 155–84.

— (1963–4) 'Proofs and Refutations', *British Journal for the Philosophy of Science*, vol. 14, pp. 1–25, 120–39, 221–45, 296–342.

— (1970) 'Falsification and the Methodology of Scientific Research Programmes', in Lakatos and Musgrave (1970) pp. 91–195.

— (1971) 'History of Science and its Rational Reconstructions', in R. C. Buck and R. S. Cohen, eds, *Boston Studies in the Philosophy of Science*, vol. 8, Dordrecht, Netherlands: Reidel, pp. 91–136.

— and Musgrave, A., eds (1970) *Criticism and the Growth of Knowledge*, Cambridge University Press.

Lancaster, K. J. (1966) 'A New Approach to Consumer Theory', *Journal of Political Economy*, vol. 74, pp. 132–57.

Lindbeck, A. (1970) 'Paul Anthony Samuelson's Contributions to Economics', *Swedish Journal of Economics*, vol. 72, pp. 342–54.

Lipsey, R. G. and Rosenbluth, G. (1971) 'A Contribution to the New Theory of Demand: A Rehabilitation of the Giffen Good', *Canadian Journal of Economics*, vol. 4, pp. 131–63.

Little, I. M. D. (1949) 'A Reformulation of the Theory of Consumer's Behaviour', *Oxford Economic Papers*, vol. 1, pp. 90–9.

— (1950) *A Critique of Welfare Economics*, Oxford: Clarendon Press, 2nd ed., 1957.

MacCrimmon, K. R. and Toda, M. (1969) 'The Experimental Determination of Indifference Curves', *Review of Economic Studies*, vol. 36, pp. 433–51.

McFadden, D. (1975) 'The Revealed Preferences of a Government Bureaucracy: Theory', *Bell Journal of Economics*, vol. 6, pp. 401–16.

— (1976) 'The Revealed Preferences of a Government Bureaucracy: Empirical Evidence', *Bell Journal of Economics*, vol. 7, pp. 55–72.

Machlup, F. (1940) 'Professor Hicks' Statics', *Quarterly Journal of Economics*, vol. 54, pp. 277–97.

— (1964) 'Professor Samuelson on Theory and Realism', *American Economic Review*, vol. 54, pp. 733–6.

Majumdar, T. (1958) *The Measurement of Utility*, London: Macmillan.

Marshall, A. (1920) *Principles of Economics*, 8th ed., London: Macmillan.

Massey, G. J. (1965) 'Professor Samuelson on Theory and Realism: Comment', *American Economic Review*, vol. 55, pp. 1155–64.

Mastermann, M. (1970) 'The Nature of a Paradigm', in Lakatos and Musgrave (1970) pp. 59–89.

Mishan, E. J. (1961) 'Theories of Consumer's Behaviour: A Cynical View', *Economica*, vol. 28, pp. 1–11.

Morgenstern, O. (1941) 'Professor Hicks on Value and Capital', *Journal of Political Economy*, vol. 49, pp. 361–93.

— (1972a) 'Thirteen Critical Points in Contemporary Economic Theory: An Interpretation', *Journal of Economic Literature*, vol. 10, pp. 1163–89.

— (1972b) 'Descriptive, Predictive, and Normative Theory', *Kyklos*, vol. 25, pp. 699–714.

Mossin, A. (1972) 'A Mean Demand Function and Individual Demand Functions Confronted with the Weak and the Strong Axioms of Revealed Preference: An Empirical Test', *Econometrica*, vol. 40, pp. 177–92.

Murakami, Y. (1968) *Logic and Social Choice*, London: Routledge & Kegan Paul.

141

Bibliography

Myrdal, G. (1932) *Das politische Element in der nationalökomischen Doctrinbildung*, Berlin: Junker und Dunnhaupt Verlag; translated by Paul Streeten as *The Political Element in the Development of Economic Theory*, London: Routledge & Kegan Paul, 1953.

Nagel, E. (1961) *The Structure of Science*, London: Routledge & Kegan Paul.

Newman, P. K. (1960a) 'Complete Ordering and Revealed Preference', *Review of Economic Studies*, vol. 27, pp. 65–77.

— (1960b) 'A Supplementary Note', *Review of Economic Studies*, vol. 27, pp. 202–5.

— (1965) *The Theory of Exchange*, Englewood Cliffs, N.J.: Prentice-Hall.

O'Neill, J., ed. (1973) *Modes of Individualism and Collectivism*, London: Heinemann.

Pareto, V. (1909) *Manuel d'économie politique*, Paris: Giard, 2nd ed., 1927.

Passmore, J. (1966) *A Hundred Years of Philosophy*, 2nd ed., London: Duckworth.

Popper, K. R. (1935) *Logik der Forschung*, Vienna: Springer Verlag; translated as *The Logic of Scientific Discovery*, London: Hutchinson, 2nd ed., 1968.

— (1945) *The Open Society and its Enemies*, 2 vols, London: Routledge; 4th ed., Routledge & Kegan Paul, 1962.

— (1956) 'Three Views Concerning Human Knowledge', in H. D. Lewis, ed., *Contemporary British Philosophy*, 3rd series, London: Allen & Unwin, pp. 355–88; as reprinted in Popper (1963a) pp. 97–119.

— (1957a) *The Poverty of Historicism*, London: Routledge & Kegan Paul, 2nd ed., 1960.

— (1957b) 'The Aim of Science', *Ratio*, vol. 1, pp. 24–35.

— (1963a) *Conjectures and Refutations*, London: Routledge & Kegan Paul, 3rd ed., 1969.

— (1963b) 'The Demarcation Between Science and Metaphysics', in P. A. Schilpp, ed., *The Philosophy of Rudolf Carnap*, La Salle, Ill.: Open Court, pp. 183–226.

— (1968a) 'Epistemology without a Knowing Subject', in B. van Rootselaar and J. F. Staal, eds, *Logic, Methodology and Philosophy of Science*, Amsterdam: North-Holland, vol. 3, pp. 333–73; as reprinted in Popper (1972) pp. 106–152.

— (1968b) 'On the Theory of the Objective Mind', *Proceedings of the XIV International Congress of Philosophy*, Vienna: University of Vienna Verlag Herder, vol. 1, pp. 25–53; as reprinted in Popper (1972) pp. 153–90.

— (1972) *Objective Knowledge*, Oxford: Clarendon Press.

Quine, W. V. O. (1951) 'Two Dogmas of Empiricism', *Philosophical Review*, vol. 60, pp. 20–43; as reprinted in W. V. Quine, *From a Logical Point of View*, New York: Harper & Row, 1961, pp. 20–46.

Richter, M. K. (1966) 'Revealed Preference Theory', *Econometrica*, vol. 34, pp. 635–45.

— (1971) 'Rational Choice', in Chipman *et al.* (1971) pp. 29–58.

Robbins, L. (1935) *An Essay on the Nature and Significance of Economic Science*, 2nd ed., London: Macmillan.

Robertson, D. H. (1951) 'Utility and All That', *Manchester School*, vol. 19. pp. 111–42.

Robinson, J. (1962) *Economic Philosophy*, London: Watts.

Roy, R. (1942) *De l'Utilité, contribution à la théorie des choix*, Paris: Hermann.

Samuelson, P. A. (1938a) 'A Note on the Pure Theory of Consumer's Behaviour', *Economica*, vol. 5, pp. 61–71.

— (1938b) 'A Note on the Pure Theory of Consumer's Behaviour: An Addendum', *Economica*, vol. 5, pp. 353–4.

— (1938c) 'The Empirical Implications of Utility Analysis', *Econometrica*, vol. 6, pp. 344–56.
— (1947) *Foundations of Economic Analysis*, Harvard University Press.
— (1948) 'Consumption Theory in Terms of Revealed Preference', *Economica*, vol. 15, pp. 243–53.
— (1950a) 'Evaluation of Real National Income', *Oxford Economic Papers*, vol. 2, pp. 1–29.
— (1950b) 'The Problem of Integrability in Utility Theory', *Economica*, vol. 17, pp. 355–85.
— (1952) 'Economic Theory and Mathematics – An Appraisal', *American Economic Review*, Papers and Proceedings, vol. 42, pp. 56–66.
— (1953) 'Consumption Theorems in Terms of Overcompensation rather than Indifference Comparisons', *Economica*, vol. 20, pp. 1–9.
— (1963) 'Problems of Methodology – Discussion', *American Economic Review*, Papers and Proceedings, vol. 53, pp. 231–6.
— (1964) 'Theory and Realism: A Reply', *American Economic Review*, vol. 54, pp. 736–9.
— (1965a) 'Professor Samuelson on Theory and Realism: Reply', *American Economic Review*, vol. 55, pp. 1164–72.
— (1965b) 'Some Notions on Causality and Teleology in Economics', in D. Lerner, ed., *Cause and Effect*, New York: Free Press, pp. 99–143.
— (1972) 'Maximum Principles in Analytical Economics', *American Economic Review*, vol. 62, pp. 249–62.
Schlesinger, G. (1963) *Method in the Physical Sciences*, London: Routledge & Kegan Paul.
Schumpeter, J. A. (1954) *History of Economic Analysis*, New York: Oxford University Press.
Sen, A. K. (1969) 'Quasi-Transitivity, Rational Choice and Collective Decisions', *Review of Economic Studies*, vol. 36, pp. 381–93.
— (1970) *Collective Choice and Social Welfare*, San Francisco: Holden-Day.
— (1971) 'Choice Functions and Revealed Preference', *Review of Economic Studies*, vol. 38, pp. 307–17.
— (1973) *Behaviour and the Concept of Preference: An Inaugural Lecture*, London School of Economics and Political Science; also reprinted in *Economica*, 1973, vol. 40, pp. 241–59.
— (1974) 'Choice, Orderings and Morality', in S. Korner, ed., *Practical Reason*, Oxford: Basil Blackwell, pp. 54–67.
Shackle, G. L. S. (1967) *The Years of High Theory*, Cambridge University Press.
— (1972) *Epistemics and Economics*, Cambridge University Press.
Slutsky, E. E. (1915) 'Sulla Teoria del Bilancio del Consumatore', *Giornale degli Economisti*, vol. 51, pp. 1–26; translated by O. Ragusa as 'On the Theory of the Budget of the Consumer', in G. J. Stigler and K. E. Boulding, eds, *Readings in Price Theory*, Homewood, Ill.: Irwin, pp. 27–56.
Stigler, G. J. (1947) 'Notes on the History of Giffen's Paradox', *Journal of Political Economy*, vol. 55, pp. 152–6.
— (1950) 'The Development of Utility Theory', *Journal of Political Economy*, vol. 58, pp. 307–27, 373–96.
— (1966) *The Theory of Price*, 3rd ed., New York: Macmillan.
Stigum, B. P. (1973) 'Revealed Preference – A Proof of Houthakker's Theorem', *Econometrica*, vol. 41, pp. 411–23.
Sweezy, A. R. (1934) 'The Interpretation of Subjective Value Theory in the Writings of the Austrian Economists', *Review of Economic Studies*, vol. 1, pp. 176–85.

Bibliography

Uzawa, H. (1960) 'Preference and Rational Choice in the Theory of Consumption', in K. J. Arrow, S. Karlin and P. Suppes, eds, *Mathematical Methods in the Social Sciences*, Stanford University Press, pp. 129–48.

Vandermeulen, D. C. (1972) 'Upward Sloping Demand Curves Without the Giffen Paradox', *American Economic Review*, vol. 62, pp. 453–8.

Ville, J. (1946) 'Sur les conditions d'existence d'une ophémlimité totale et d'un indice du niveau des prix', *Annales de l' Université de Lyon*, vol. 9, pp. 32–9; translated by P. K. Newman as 'The Existence Conditions of a Total Utility Function', *Review of Economic Studies*, 1951–2, vol. 19, pp. 123–8.

Viner, J. (1925) 'The Utility Concept in Value Theory and Its Critics', *Journal of Political Economy*, vol. 33, pp. 369–87, 638–59.

Watkins, J. W. N. (1957) 'Between Analytic and Empirical', *Philosophy*, vol. 32, pp. 112–31.

— (1958) 'Confirmable and Influential Metaphysics', *Mind*, vol. 67, pp. 344–65.

— (1960) 'When are Statements Empirical?', *British Journal for the Philosophy of Science*, vol. 10, pp. 287–308.

— (1965) *Hobbes's System of Ideas*, London: Hutchinson.

Wicksell, K. (1919) 'Professor Cassels nationalekonomiska System', *Ekonomisk Tidskrift*, vol. 21, pp. 195–226; translated by Solomon Adler in K. Wicksell, *Lectures on Political Economy*, London: Routledge, 1934, vol. 1, pp. 219–57.

Wold, H. O. A. (1951) 'Demand Functions and the Integrability Conditions', *Skandinavisk Aktuarietidskrift*, vol. 34, pp. 149–51.

— and L. Juréen (1953) *Demand Analysis*, New York: Wiley.

Wong, S. (1973) 'The "F-Twist" and the Methodology of Paul Samuelson', *American Economic Review*, vol. 63, pp. 312–25.

Name Index

145

Name index

Jarvie, I. C., 130–1
Jevons, W. S., 14, 22

Katzner, D. W., 1
Kelvin, W. T., 108
Kepler, J., 107, 115–16
Kihlstrom, R., 47
Knight, F. H., 107
Koo, A. Y. C., 133, 135
Kornai, J., 61, 82
Koyré, A., 131
Kuhn, T. S., 130, 132

Lakatos, I., 115, 130–2, 134–5
Lancaster, K. J., 129
Lindbeck, A., 130
Lipsey, R. G., 132
Little, I. M. D., 14, 64, 67, 69, 79, 87, 100, 129, 135

MacCrimmon, K. R., 85, 133
McFadden, D., 86
Mach, E., 135
Machlup, F., 33, 107
Majumdar, T., 135
Marshall, A., 14, 25–30, 33–5, 38, 41–43, 45, 50–1, 132
Mas-Colell, A., 47
Massey, G. J., 108, 117, 130, 136
Mastermann, M., 130
Mayer, H., 131
Menger, C., 106
Mill, J. S., 17, 131
Mises, L. von, 107
Mishan, E. J., 86
Morgenstern, O., 33, 130
Mossin, A., 135
Murakami, Y., 135
Musgrave, A., 132
Myrdal, G., 129

Nagel, E., 107, 113–14, 130, 136
Neumann, J. von, 130
Newman, P. K., 1, 57, 129, 136
Newton, I., 107, 115–16, 130

O'Neill, J., 131

Pareto, V., 2, 13–14, 17, 22, 25, 27–8, 30, 33–5, 50, 111, 118, 132
Passmore, J., 107
Pattanaik, P. K., 133
Popper, K. R., 10, 20, 57, 113–16, 121, 130–7

Quandt, R. G., 84, 89, 132
Quine, W. V. O., 135

Richter, M. K., 4, 47, 59–60, 86, 129, 136
Robbins, L., 14, 48, 107, 131
Robertson, D. H., 2
Robinson, J., 2, 17, 82, 132
Rosenbluth, G., 132
Roy, R., 12

Schlesinger, G., 57, 131
Schumpeter, J. A., 18, 33, 102, 129
Sen, A. K., 2, 58–60, 86, 90, 92, 97–8, 131, 133–4, 136
Shackle, G. L. S., 13, 22, 31, 33, 41–2, 131
Slutsky, E. E., 2, 42, 44, 54, 111, 118, 129
Sonnenschein, H., 47
Sraffa, P., 135
Stigler, G. J., 42, 129, 132, 134
Stigum, B. P., 129, 136
Strigl, R., 131
Sweezy, A. R., 6, 48, 129, 131

Toda, M., 85, 133

Uzawa, H., 5, 6, 47, 86, 129, 136

Vandermeulen, D. C., 132
Ville, J., 136
Viner, J., 129, 132–3

Walras, L., 28
Watkins, J. W. N., 130, 136
Wicksell, K., 129
Wieser, F. von, 131
Wold, H. O. A., 6
Wong, S., 129–30, 132, 135

Subject Index